TOO BROWN TO KEEP

A Search for Love, Forgiveness, and Healing

by Judy Fambrough-Billingsley

ISBN: 978-0-578-44002-6

Reona L. James

DEDICATION

To Mama and Daddy,
whose encouragement, life lessons, and love
empowered me
to always do my best.
I love you to the moon and back.
Thank you for adopting me.

TABLE OF CONTENTS

ACKNOWLEDGMENTS

Thank you to all who helped me on my journey to discovery and healing:

My sons, Chris and Chad, who were the recipients of my young, inexperienced parenting; my two beautiful daughters-in-law, Tana and Casey; and my grandsons, Matthew, Devin, and Cameron. Their love and encouragement to write the book sustained me beyond measure.

I am grateful to my sisters JoAnn and Tammi for their unconditional love and support.

To my newly discovered family; Earl, Hannelore, Reinhard, Fritz, Jürgen, Helga, Ernst, and all the villagers of Bingenheim, Germany I am truly blessed to have you in my life.

AUTHOR'S NOTE

Unanswered questions began to surface during my elementary school days when teachers gave us writing assignments centered on our family, our parents, and our life experiences. I was reminded how little I knew about myself every time I went to the doctor or dentist and family health history questions went unanswered as the nurse marked "Unknown" on the questionnaire.

It was only once I began to wonder *Who am I?* and try to figure out my purpose in life that I began to question what early life experiences in Germany had contributed to my basic foundation as a human being. *What was life truly like in Germany with my mother, father, and sisters? Did my early years in Germany contribute in any way to my substance as a human being today?* There was a hole in my sense of being that ran deep and cloudy with doubt and guilt that I somehow was the cause of my mother's abandoning all of us to a life of uncertainty. *Am I to blame for breaking up the family? Was my skin too dark? Was my hair too woolly? Was I an embarrassment to her? Did she love me?*

I have no recollection of my life before growing up in the United States. The story of my early German childhood years relies heavily on eyewitness accounts; my adoption papers; personal letters; photographs; the recollections of various members of my original German family, neighbors, and fellow villagers; and the orphanage in which I found myself at the tender age of two.

Factual evidence and supporting documents, along with the personal interviews I conducted during my many trips to Germany, form the foundation for re-creating the story of my earliest years, my stay in the Kinderheim (orphanage), and my eventual adoption.

Putting the puzzle pieces of my life together and discovering the answers to many of my questions provided me with the tools necessary to deal with the feeling of "less than" that often crept into my mind whenever I thought about my adoption. Finally, the missing pieces of my personal patchwork life-quilt would calm the restlessness I had always felt throughout my life and replace it with a sense of belonging.

When you discover, address, and accept your ancestry in all respects, you will have acquired much of the information you need in order to answer the question *Who am I?* It is not your reaction to the discovery but what you do with it that will determine a positive or negative outcome. I wish you well on your journey to self-discovery.

CHAPTER I

ELSE'S PLAN

"They say that abandonment is a wound that never heals. I say only that an abandoned child never forgets."
—*Mario Balotelli*

Imgard and I were excited, each holding one of our grown-up friend Gertrud's hands as she guided us out Mrs. Webber's front door. The gathering clouds of the morning had thickened and darkened. They now looked heavy with rain.

To Imgard, at five years old, and me, just short of two and a half, the threat of a downpour meant only one thing: an early end to our happy day of playing outdoors. Already our babysitter, Mrs. Webber, was laying our friend Wolfgang down for his nap inside the house. My sister and I felt fortunate to be coming back outside to run and play a little longer.

"Come, Ute, Imgard," Gertrud said, gripping our hands securely as she walked with us across Mrs. Webber's little patch of front lawn, so lushly green under the leaden sky. Imgard and I skipped along the bumpy dirt road that was the main thoroughfare through our tiny village, prattling to each other about what we would do once we reached the church grounds.

A few sprinkles of rain pricked our grubby faces and painted dark pockmarks on the dust beneath our feet. Gertrud held on to us tightly as we pulled at her hands, yelling, "Faster! Let's walk faster!" At our innocent ages, we did not question why we would be heading out for more play in the churchyard rather than staying indoors when the heavens were about to break open and drench us to the skin.

As we passed our own house, or our apartment rather, just a few yards from our babysitter Mrs. Webber's, we saw our older sister Helga gazing out the window, her face flushed, tears streaming down her cheeks. Only then did we take notice that Helga had not joined us in our afternoon play but had stayed home with our mother, Else. Delighted that we were the ones outside, and blithely unconcerned about Helga's plight, Imgard and I waved to her. "Hi, Helga!" we shouted as we skipped by the window. No doubt she was disappointed at not being allowed to join us outdoors.

The village church was a very short distance away from our flat. In fact, you could stand out in front of the house where we lived and clearly see the church's large wooden double doors. As the three of us reached the churchyard, my sister and I glanced back. Our mother was standing on the dirt road, arms crossed, watching us. Eager to take our chance to play before she might call us home, Imgard and I pulled away from Gertrud's unresisting hands and began to chase each other across the spacious lawn while Gertrud watched, near at hand, and our mother, too, stood silently in the distance.

After perhaps a few minutes, a gleaming black Cadillac rounded a curve and cruised slowly up the road. Finally it crept to a stop along the church grounds, right in front of where we were playing. My sister and I stopped our running, curious to see who was in the big, imposing car. Imgard knew the vehicle didn't belong to anyone who lived in our village.

"Who's that?" I asked Imgard. She shrugged her shoulders and grabbed my hand. I glanced up at her. She was frowning.

"What's wrong, Imgard?" I asked as she pulled me closer, wrapping her arms around me while her eyes locked onto the woman who was stepping out from the driver's seat. The raindrops were larger now, our hair and shabby dresses grown cool and damp. The woman walked around the car, flung the back door open, and gestured with her hands for both of us to get in the backseat.

Imgard began to back away, and I with her, but Gertrud came and again took our hands.

"Come on, children," said the stranger next to the car, "nothing to be afraid of. We're going for a nice drive in the country. We can stop and get ice cream on the way! Come now . . ."

The lady walked toward us as Gertrud led us to her. Imgard's arms and legs stiffened with resistance as the unfamiliar woman lifted her up and deposited her in the backseat. Then Gertrud picked me up and handed me over to the lady, who placed me in the backseat next to a very frightened Imgard, who had begun to cry. Tears streamed down her face as the massive black Cadillac's door closed and locked. Imgard pressed her face against the window and screamed as loudly as she could, banging both fists on the glass in a desperate effort to bring attention to our plight.

Gertrud stepped away from the car. The lady got back in,

started the car, and set it in motion, again promising us ice cream if we behaved.

I snuggled up against Imgard as close as possible, knowing that something about the situation was not right. I craned my head to look for our mother. No sign of her. She wouldn't like us to get into a car with a perfect stranger. Imgard kept one arm around me as she continued to weep, and because she wept, I cried, too.

The car exited the village. Rain now pounded on the hood and slithered in rivulets down the windows. The windshield wipers came on. *Thump . . . thump . . . thump . . .*

Although upset and disoriented, I was too young to understand the peril that Imgard knew in her gut: that we were in a strange car in the company of a stranger who was taking us away forever from our mother, our sister, our friends, and the only home we had ever known.

CHAPTER II

AN ERA OF RACISM

*"We must not allow other people's limited
perceptions to define us."*
—*Virginia Satir*

Germany and the United States, along with many civilians working behind the scenes, made life-altering decisions based solely on the racial ideology that existed in Germany at the time of my birth. For the thousands of us who were abandoned by our birth mothers, Germany's racial beliefs and biases took precedence over consideration of what would be in the best interest of the child.

My birth on October 1, 1950, in the hospital of Friedberg, Germany, occurred during an atmosphere of ongoing racial tension and division that had begun before World War I. Despite interracial marriages being legal in Germany before the turn of the century, there was still a belief among many that the mixing of races should be discouraged. When the First World War ended, in 1918, French occupying forces included African colonial troops, a number of whom fathered children with German women. False stories began to circulate, reported by newspapers, that these German women had been raped rather than the relationships' having been consensual, despite locals often describing these troops as polite and even well liked.

In the early 1920s, Adolf Hitler joined what would shortly become the Nazi Party and began to stir things up with revolution in mind. It failed, and he ended up in prison, convicted of high treason. It was then that he authored his infamous two-volume manifesto, *Mein Kampf*, or *My Struggle*, in which he laid out his plans to transform Germany into a society based on the Aryan race, which he deemed pure, authentic, and superior. Hitler assured the Germans that they were destined to rule all other races. He warned that the blending of pure Aryan blood with that of other races would weaken the "master race," causing a decline and the eventual downfall of Germany. In his book, he described mixed-race children as a contamination of the white race. He accused Jews of wanting to bring "Negroes into the Rhineland" with the idea of "bastardizing the white race" so that Jews could weaken the population and ultimately take control of Germany.

By the early 1930s, Hitler had secured 36 percent of the vote in running for president and was named chancellor. By 1933, he managed to disenfranchise all the other political parties and become the head of state. He went on to introduce the Nuremberg Laws, which, among other things, banned marriages between German Jews and non-Jews and facilitated the persecution of Jews, leading to the start of World War II in 1939. While Jews were the main target, Hitler's regime also singled out other groups: Communists, Social Democrats, Socialists, Poles, homosexuals, Jehovah's Witnesses, Africans, and Rom, or gypsies, all of whom were targeted for internment and likely death in the Nazi-run concentration camps.

Although Germany was ultimately defeated in that World

War, Hitler's ideology of racial purity and distrust remained a firm belief among many Germans. Grappling with their country's devastating loss, they held fast to their idea that the physical characteristics of a pure German Aryan race meant blond hair, blue eyes, and fair skin. All others were the enemy.

Needless to say, I, with a biological father who was black, did not fit into that category, although Imgard resembled my mother, with her fair complexion, blonde hair, and hazel eyes, as did my oldest half-sister, Helga, who was not my father's child. That said, Imgard and I still possessed German birth certificates, granting the two of us full German citizenship.

Nazi Germany was by no means the only country spouting racist ideas and actions. After the Civil War in the United States, the Thirteenth Amendment to the Constitution abolished slavery in 1865. The Fourteenth Amendment, ratified in 1868, gave blacks equal protection under the law, and two years later, the Fifteenth Amendment granted them voting rights.

And yet, despite these measures, especially in the southern states, the lynching and killing of blacks continued. Discrimination against blacks gained new legal cover with the introduction of Jim Crow laws, which required segregation not only of housing but in all realms, thanks to the 1896 Supreme Court ruling that decreed that facilities for blacks and whites must be equal but could be legally kept separate: separate bathrooms and water fountains, separate seating on buses and in eating establishments, and separation in any public place, even schools and municipal swimming pools. By law, blacks had to give up their place to any white person if and when all available seats were taken. All based solely on the color of one's skin. Not until the 1950s and '60s did the civil rights movement force the United States to begin implementing equal rights for African Americans.

Millions of black men registered for the draft and served as draftees or volunteers in all branches of the US armed forces during World War II, and were subject to racial discrimination and segregation, with most serving in noncombat roles, such as cooks, quartermasters, maintenance mechanics, and gravediggers, because they were not allowed to fight alongside white soldiers.

My biological father, Earl Laughton, served as a vehicle maintenance mechanic for the US Army while stationed in Germany. The African American soldier stationed in Europe during World War II experienced a level of freedom and acceptance among Europeans that generally did not exist in the United States. In Europe, my father was safe from Jim Crow laws and the risk of lynching that existed in the United States. Of his thirty-five years of service in the army, he spent fifteen stationed in Germany.

"I loved Germany. I had a lot of freedom over there that Negro men didn't have in the United States," he later told me. "I felt much more accepted in Germany than I ever did at home. That was a time when Negroes were treated as human beings in Europe, much more so than here."

Many African American soldiers, like Earl, ignored the military rules against fraternization that warned soldiers not to become too friendly with the Germans. Many German women engaged in romantic affairs with, and in some cases married, African American soldiers. As a result, thousands of "brown babies" were born in and out of wedlock during and immediately following World War II, despite Germany's lingering belief in the importance of racial purity.

Children of these unions, like my sister Imgard and me, were often called *de Besatzungskindern*, occupation children, as our fathers were among the occupying forces. Less accepting Germans referred to us with a far more derogatory moniker, *Mischlingskinder*, half-breed children, a term first used to single out children born to Jewish-German parents. There was no place in German society for *Mischlingskinder*, and both governments, German and American, viewed them as a problem that must be resolved after the war ended.

Although both governments focused primarily on the offspring of US soldiers, some German women had children by soldiers stationed there from other countries, namely France and its colonies Algeria, Morocco, Tunisia, and French Indochina. The US military's policy at the time was to reject any claims of paternity made by German mothers. As my father shared with me many years later, it was rare that the United States military would allow the marriage of an African American soldier to a white German woman. Soldiers needed permission from their commanding officers, and the women often had to undergo a series of mental and physical tests. African American soldiers who wanted to marry their white girlfriends were often moved to other military bases many miles away.

I interviewed a number of African American veterans who served in Germany with my father during World War II. Over lunch in the commissary at New Jersey's Fort Dix, all shared similar stories of how the army discouraged them from maintaining permanent relationships with German women.

A few of the veterans at the table, including my father, had nonetheless married German women by exploiting a brief period of civilian status between the time their enlistment ended and when they received approval to reenlist. By the time reenlistment took effect, these soldiers, now married, claimed their spouses on their reenlistment papers and eventually relocated to the United States, where they raised their families.

Other US servicemen in similar situations chose instead to leave the mothers of their children and go on to marry American women upon returning home. "Too much paperwork," one veteran chuckled. "If you weren't careful, you might one day receive an order that you were being reassigned to another base immediately or sent back to the US," another said.

It was a difficult time for biracial children to be born in the 1950s, shortly after the war had ended. The racial divide and biases had not subsided but were very much alive and well in both Germany and the United States. The war had not stamped out the racial tensions that existed in both countries. Neither country was willing to take full responsibility for the existence of thousands of mixed-race children born to German women and African American soldiers. Many mixed-race children became collateral damage from the ravages of the war in Germany. In most cases, we were babies without a country, whom no one wanted.

CHAPTER III

LIFE IN THE VILLAGE

"Parenthood requires love, not DNA."
—*Source unknown*

Bingenheim Ezchell, Germany, where Imgard and I lived our earliest years, is a quaint, quiet village dating back to the eleventh century. Set in the western part of the country in Hesse, one of Germany's federal states, it is located forty-five minutes south of Frankfurt am Main (Frankfurt on the Main River), away from any hint of city life.

The village's most prominent feature is the sixteenth-century Bingenheim Castle, which stands majestically against a crystal blue country sky, its ample grounds of lush green grass providing grazing for village livestock. The castle's tower is infamous for being home to one of Germany's four largest witch trials, the Witch Trials of Fulda, 1603–6, which resulted in the deaths of approximately 250 people.

Bingenheim Castle Tower

Today, all that remains of the castle is the ruins of the execution tower and portions of the exterior stone wall winding about a quarter of a mile along the now-dried-up moat that once protected the perimeter. These days, instead of water, the former moat is pastoral in appearance, covered in verdant and floral vegetation, its tranquility hiding any sign of its violent past.

Although refurbished since my life in the village, the Evangelische Kirchengemeinde Protestant church was built in

the 1800s. Its tall, grand steeple with its modern clock is distinctive against the dark shake roof and pure white stucco exterior walls. The steeple houses the church bell, which chimes daily every hour and beckons the villagers to worship on Sundays. A fork in the road splits the entrance and exit, extending a welcome to all

Bingenheim Village Church

who enter and a "come back soon" to all who are leaving.

It was in this homey little village that I lived as a newborn in 1950 with my then-29-year-old mother, Else née Claassen Schaab.

Else herself was born on May 2, 1921, to Liba Kuschelewitsch-Claassen and Rudolf Claassen. Little is known about Else's French father, Rudolf Claassen, who was born in Metz, northeastern France, near the borders of Germany and Luxembourg. Else's mother, Liba Kuschelewitsch, an

Ashkenazi Jew, was born in the town of Riga, Latvia. The Ashkenazi Jews originated in Eastern Europe and, according to genealogies of the Hebrew Bible, were descendants of Noah. Sometime during her adolescence, Liba's family moved to Lublin, Poland, where she was raised. As an adult, she moved to Frankfurt am Main, Germany, where she met and married Rudolf, who became an alcoholic and beat her whenever he got drunk.

In 1933, Hitler and the Nazi Party began taking steps to institutionalize the persecution of German Jewish citizens. When Germany invaded Poland, the Nazis shot and killed thousands of Polish Jews, confined others to ghettoes where they starved to death, and sent thousands to death camps throughout Poland. Unlike concentration camps, which were created to detain Jews, political prisoners, and other perceived enemies of the Nazi state, death camps existed for the sole purpose of killing Jews and other "undesirables," in what became known as the Holocaust.

The death camps were integral to Hitler's plan to exterminate all Jews, as millions died from malnutrition, disease, and overwork, or were immediately executed upon their arrival. The "Final Solution" to the "Jewish problem" was the systematic murder of all European Jews. Hitler was convinced that his problem would be resolved only with the elimination of every Jew under his control, along with artists, educators, Rom, Communists, homosexuals, the mentally and physically handicapped, and others who were deemed unfit to live in Nazi Germany.

Born with blonde hair (that would later turn dark brown) and hazel eyes, Else could pass as a member of Hitler's Aryan race. Given her maternal Jewish ancestry, these characteristics were particularly important assets that allowed her to survive Hitler's murderous reign. The brutal race-bashing she witnessed was etched in her soul forever when she watched Nazi soldiers forcibly remove her Jewish mother from their home, whisking her away to work and ultimately die in a concentration camp.

The last enduring memory Else had of that event was of her beautiful, beloved mother being brutally shoved by Nazi soldiers into a truck full of sobbing Jewish women and stone-faced Jewish men who were being forcibly transported to a concentration camp. An agonized Liba could do nothing as she witnessed her daughter sprinting after the truck, screaming at the top of her lungs, "Mutter! Mutter!" ("Mother!"), as the truck quickly picked up speed and barreled down the narrow Frankfurt street. Realizing that it was hopeless, Else surrendered to the inevitable, sobbing uncontrollably as she walked back to her father, who stood in the middle of the road in front of their home.

Liba Kuschelewitsch-Claassen
Else's Mother

Rudolf Claassen was permitted to continue working on the Deutsche Reichsbahn, the German Reich railway, while raising his half-Jewish daughter. The government gave him permission to keep Else with the strict condition that he raise her as a German non-Jew. Her father was very much aware that the Gestapo, Nazi Germany's secret police, would keep a watchful eye on him, alert for any minor transgression that would result in his making the same trip as his wife to the dreaded concentration camp.

After Liba's internment, Else was left to care for herself and her alcoholic father. Returning home from school one afternoon, Else prepared dinner, as she had done daily since her mother's departure. Waiting patiently for her father to return home from work, she did some light housekeeping and began doing her homework. Else expected and waited, but her father never came home from work—not that evening or the next. Rudolf never returned to the house that he had shared with his daughter. It was rumored that he returned to Metz, France, leaving his teenage daughter to fend for herself, despite her young age and lack of financial support.

Abandoned and alone, Else was forced to quickly become a strong, independent, self-sufficient young woman. Though she had little education, she worked in factories and in low-paying domestic jobs before, during, and after the war. She managed to hold a variety of positions throughout her life, but one was especially significant: living and working for the Webber family in Bingenheim.

Else moved from Frankfurt to Bingenheim around 1940, during World War II. There she found domestic work helping her neighbor, Mrs. Webber, who lived across the street. Mrs. Webber and Else became close in what eventually grew into a lifelong friendship as they became an integral part of each other's life.

Mrs. Webber suffered from severe arthritis pain and increasingly required a doctor's care. She could no longer complete all the necessary household chores. Else became her caregiver and housekeeper, as well as nanny to the Webbers' six children, and regularly accompanied Mrs. Webber to the doctor for weekly water-therapy treatments.

Else felt safe living among the villagers, especially in light of the deep and loving friendship she had with Mrs. Webber and her family. Being among friends and living in the village so far away from Frankfurt reassured Else that it was highly unlikely that anyone would suspect that she was half Jewish. No longer lonely, yet not knowing what the next day might bring, Else felt reasonably safe, a real part of the Webber family.

Else 1940

Over the years, Else had grown into an attractive young lady. She was a young, slender German beauty, five feet five inches tall, with hazel eyes and shoulder-length, curly, dark-brown hair. Feeling safe enough to venture out, Else decided it was time to focus on marriage, having a family, and bringing happiness into her life.

Not having had a good role model while growing up, she didn't have any idea what to look for in a husband. Memories of her parents' physical interactions made her determined not to make the same mistake her mother had in choosing an abusive man. What Else did know for certain was that she was going to do all she could to avoid being with men like her father.

Else's first great love, as well as her greatest secret, was a handsome and charismatic Nazi German soldier serving in

World War II. Focused on his promising career, he quickly rose up the military ladder of success. In the early 1940s, Else found herself pregnant with his child. She was ecstatic and couldn't wait to share the good news with the man she adored and hoped to marry. She had planned to spend the rest of her life with him, supporting his efforts to one day be a part of Hitler's regime. She tried to look as coy and beautiful as she could when she shared the news with her lover. To her utter disappointment, he informed her that marrying a half-Jewish woman would put his career in ruins. He had no intention or desire to marry her.

Months later, devastated and alone, Else gave birth to her firstborn child in a Frankfurt hospital. Three days after the birth, having named her newborn son Ernst Claassen (name changed to protect his privacy), she relinquished all parental rights to the state and quietly walked away from her three-day-old son, determined to leave all memory of him behind.

Several years later, Else met Ferdinand Schaab, a veteran and invalid thirty-three years her senior. This was her first marriage. She married Ferdinand, hoping he would financially support her after she had worked hard for so many years to make ends meet. The struggle was genuine for Else, as she had found a variety of low-paying factory jobs that did not pay enough for her to adequately feed and clothe herself. For her, sheer survival from paycheck to paycheck was a daunting task that took much of her energy and sapped her spirit.

At the age of twenty-three, Else gave birth to a healthy baby girl, Helga Schaab, on June 10, 1944, in Frankfurt am Main Hospital shortly after getting married. Else felt a particular responsibility to make her second pregnancy work.

This was her opportunity to prove she could be a good mother. After all, this baby was legitimate; Else was a married woman. Helga's father, Ferdinand, was fifty-five at the time and in failing mental health. He was diagnosed with combat fatigue (today known as post-traumatic stress disorder) from his having served in World War I and World War II. Shortly after Helga's birth, Ferdinand tried unsuccessfully to hang himself with a rope tied to their bedroom doorknob. Else walked in just in time to save him. Ferdinand was confined to a veteran's home for long-term mental care, where he would remain until his death.

Once again, Else did not have the income to support herself and her newborn baby girl. Not knowing what else to do, Else began divorce proceedings, intent on walking away from her husband. But she stayed to raise Helga in Bingenheim, where they would both be cared for by friends and villagers who knew her well.

Else resumed her domestic jobs working for Mother Webber and other villagers, cleaning house, cooking, gardening, caregiving, and doing other odd jobs to support herself and Helga. She was grateful for any work that brought her an income to support herself and her daughter.

But life was far from comfortable in war-torn Germany, where many of the villagers had lost their jobs due to the downfall of the nation's economy. Eventually, Else could no longer rely on villagers for domestic employment. Unable to find a steady job to support herself and her young daughter, she placed Helga in a Kinderheim several hours away from the village until the young mother could financially support both of them.

In Germany, there is no stigma attached to parents who leave their children in the care of a Kinderheim while they seek stable employment and financial stability. The government and those who use the Kinderheims have an understanding that once the parent becomes financially stable, they will pick up their child and return home to become a family again.

With Helga residing temporarily in the Kinderheim, Else not only had time to look for a steady job but also gained the freedom to go out for the evening. When war ended and American troops remained stationed in Germany, Else and her girlfriends had many free evenings to flirt with US soldiers. Saturday nights meant hundreds of soldiers in Frankfurt would be out looking for fun and companionship, their wallets stuffed with cash. The war had caused a scarcity of many things, including the luxuries that women favored, like silk stockings, perfume, red lipstick, and shampoo. Even canned milk was a luxury. American soldiers had access to these items, which were plentiful and easily acquired with a military ID through the commissary store on their base. German women couldn't help but favor the soldiers who supplied them with such luxury items.

Riding along with her friends to the city, Else mingled with the servicemen, enthusiastically doing the jitterbug and dancing the swing. Her natural rhythm and ability to dance attracted admiring stares from soldiers as her shoulder-length, curly brown hair swung in time to the music. Her piercing hazel eyes sparkled with delight, her beaming smile showing perfect white teeth. One soldier in particular caught her eye: the good-looking Earl Laughton, out with his buddies for an evening of fun.

CHAPTER IV

ELSE AND EARL

"The most painful good-byes are the ones that are never said and never explained."
—*Source unknown*

Earl Laughton was born on June 16, 1926, in Norfolk, Virginia. He was the youngest of three children born to Ethel Johnson Laughton. Although Albert Laughton was not Earl's biological father, he raised him as his own, giving him the Laughton name. Earl and his two older brothers all shared the same mother. He inherited his chocolate brown skin from his parents, along with his short, black, woolly hair. He knew how to charm the ladies at a very early age with his spunky personality, his charming wit, and his laughter that allowed his white teeth to gleam through an infectious smile. Being familiar with the conditions of poverty, Earl found himself spending far more time working the farm than going to school. He eventually dropped out of school to work the family farm full-time, out of loyalty and necessity.

Earl had an adventuresome spirit that motivated him to find a career that would provide a trade while traveling the world. The merchant marine seemed attractive, and he applied, but his application was denied without reason given. Earl felt the decision stemmed from discrimination due to racism, which was prevalent in the military during the 1940s. After his rejection from the merchant marine, he enlisted in the US Army. It was during the enlistment process that Earl discovered that his original birth certificate had a modified date of birth, a different father, and a different last name than the one he had lived by for the past eighteen years.

"I never asked, and my mother never told me why that happened," Earl told me. "She didn't act concerned, nor did she ever explain how it happened. During those days, you didn't ask those types of questions of your parents. I just knew I was born out of wedlock," he explained as he laughed nervously, describing the difficulties he encountered while trying to join the army.

With help from the army, Earl's birth certificate was changed to reflect the Laughton surname he had unofficially been given and raised to believe was his by blood. His birth was corrected from April to June 16, 1926. With all legal documents in order, Earl entered the service with the agreement that he would earn his GED, a requirement in order to remain in the army. "I easily earned my high school GED while in the military, which allowed me to remain in service of my country," Earl told me, grinning with pride.

He received his basic training at Fort Dix, in New Jersey, and then transferred to Fort Eustis, in Newport News, Virginia, where he became a skilled army auto and equipment mechanic in the Transportation Corps, the mechanics division of the army. He was then sent to serve in Germany at the tail end of World War II. He and his peers were responsible for ensuring the movement of personnel and supplies by keeping all vehicles in good operating condition, which allowed them to be delivered to various base camps and to troops on the front lines. At the end of World War II, army soldiers working as transportation mechanics had contributed to the movement of more than 7 million soldiers and 126 million tons of military supplies.

Else and Earl both ignored the military rules against fraternization and the common belief that the coming together, the mixing of races, between white German women and African American soldiers would weaken the German goal of establishing a "master race." "We were both attracted to each other, and she was a pretty good dancer," Earl told me during one of many interviews with him. "We got along just fine, and we began spending more and more time together."

Once the American soldiers occupied Germany, things improved for Else. When she had first met Earl, she'd been unemployed and struggling financially. Earl entered her life just at the right time to provide companionship and lend financial support.

To those who knew the couple, Earl proved himself to be a kind and caring person in his treatment of Else. Shortly after they met, he visited her in the village for the first time. While there, he noticed a framed picture hanging on the wall above her couch. When Else revealed to him the financial hardship that had forced her to place Helga in a

Earl and Else -1950

Kinderheim, Earl told Else to bring her daughter home. He assured Else that he would help financially so that her child could live with her in Bingenheim. He was true to his word. They had become a couple.

Earl never married Else, but they did have an intimate, monogamous relationship resulting in the birth of my sister Imgard on June 29, 1947, and my own birth (with the given name Ute) three years later, on October 1, 1950. Our soldier father lived and worked on the base but tried to spend as much time as possible with us in the village. Everyone understood that his first obligation was to the United States Army. When he got time off to leave the base, he would hurriedly catch the train or hitch a ride with a fellow soldier to our house. Earl was delighted to witness our excitement as my sisters and I jumped up and down with our hands outstretched for the treats he would hand us upon arrival.

There was joy when he came to visit, as he would bring gifts—an assortment of treats, including chocolate candy bars, which were scarce to buy. The whole village knew when he had arrived and knew that many of them would be sharing in the indulgences he had brought to us, as Else often shared the treats with neighbors and friends once he returned to base. Gertrud, Mrs. Webber's daughter-in-law who lived across the street from us, recalled, "My son Wolfgang and I were so delighted to see Earl arrive at your house. We both knew that Else would share the treats with us after he had left. Your father was a good man. He always smiled and spoke to us. He was quite handsome in his military uniform," she said with a twinkle in her eye and a smile on her lips. Our father made a lasting impression on the villagers, who spoke to me with smiles and laughter as they reminisced about the times he spent in the village with them.

Arriving unannounced one sunny afternoon, Earl placed several pieces of chocolate in our hands, then gave each of us a hug. Imgard giggled as he tossed her up into the air before setting her down beside Helga. He whisked past them both as he entered the house, calling with excitement in his voice, "Else! Else!" Not finding her in the kitchen or the living room, he opened the bedroom door, spreading his arms wide in anticipation of her rushing into them. Instead, he found Else standing naked by their bed, desperately trying to gather her undergarments from the floor, while a startled neighbor hurriedly grabbed his clothing that was scattered around the room. Just as Earl rushed toward him, hauling off to punch him hard, the neighbor jumped out the bedroom window and sprinted down the dirt road in fear for his life, with Earl just steps behind him.

Earl returned to the United States, where he served out the few remaining months of his enlistment in the army at Fort Dix. Upon the completion of his reenlistment paperwork, Earl returned to Germany to learn that Else had given us up for adoption, refusing to give him any information. With no resources available to find us, Earl resigned himself to the fact he would never see us again. "My mother and I talked about looking for both of you but didn't have the money to even get started. So we just gave up hoping you would one day find us," Earl explained when I asked him why he hadn't looked for us.

Meanwhile, Else, like many other German women who had children by occupied soldiers, struggled financially to support us after her relationship with Earl had ended.

Germany's economy was still feeling the effects of World War II, which left many people out of work. Else could not find steady employment that would pay enough to support all of us. With no more financial support from Earl and no job, she quickly ran out of money.

Alone, frustrated, and unhappy, Else took her aggressions out on Imgard, often backhanding her across the face, more because of her own predicament than anything Imgard had done. Many of the villagers witnessed the physical abuse Else inflicted on my nearest sister. On several occasions, adult women, some of them mothers themselves, approached Else and offered to take on full responsibility for Imgard and raise her as their own daughter. Else refused their offers and continued her physical abuse of Imgard.

Toni, a friend to Mother Webber's daughter Hannelore, described the physical abuse she and Hannelore often witnessed Imgard experiencing at the hands of our mother. "Your mother was ugly to Imgard. She took her moods out on her. I have seen it with my own eyes. She would leave you and Helga out of it. Gertrud and I told our mother about it. She talked to Else and asked her if she would let her have Imgard."

"I realize that you are having a hard time supporting all of your children, Else," Mother Webber said. "Maybe I can help you by having Imgard live with me. This way you would only have to worry about two rather than three little girls."

"I am looking for work," Else replied firmly, "and I will soon be able to support all of us."

"Yes, you will," countered Mother Webber, "but for now, I could take Imgard off your hands. Then when you get back on your feet, Imgard could return to you and her sisters."

"I said no. I can do it myself!" Else shouted.

"All right, Else. Please remember my offer. I was just trying to help," Mother Webber said, putting a close to the discussion.

Nonetheless, Else made the fateful decision to abandon all three of her daughters, starting with Imgard and me. Realizing that many of the villagers knew of her physical abuse of Imgard I believe was one of the contributing factors that led to the decision. For Else, the pattern of abandonment was established when her father abandoned her in her teens. In her view, when life became miserable and unbearable, it was time to shed all that was connected with it and make a new start.

Having witnessed her father's way of resolving problems, Else had abandoned her firstborn child, Ernst, during World War II. Finding herself facing racism when her Nazi lover told her he could not marry a Jew, she reverted to the only action she knew: to walk away, leaving everything behind to start a new life in new surroundings. Early in the 1950s, again facing racism and financial hardship, Else abandoned her three little girls to a life of uncertainty as she began a new life on her own in Frankfurt am Main.

CHAPTER V

THE KINDERHEIM

"Being unwanted, unloved, uncared for, forgotten by everybody, I think that is a much greater hunger, a much greater poverty than a person who has nothing to eat."
Mother Teresa

Riding my tricycle in the street and playing with dolls was my daily routine when I lived in Bingenheim with my sisters Helga and Imgard; mother, Else; and father, Earl, when he could visit. We lived in a bleak, shabby, ground-level flat with one bedroom, a bathroom, a kitchen, and a living room that also served as sleeping quarters for us three girls. The central point of the flat was the living room, furnished with second-hand décor sparsely placed to accommodate the small space. Our couch was draped with an old, multicolored, thin cotton quilt that hid the cotton stuffing escaping through numerous tears in the upholstery.

The walls of the living room were dirty gray, with a few family pictures of Else with Helga and with Earl, and a single photo of Imgard and Helga, nailed on the wall over the couch. The photographs in their thin black frames were strategically placed to hide rips in the aging wallpaper. Several straight-backed chairs showing their decaying wood through chipped white paint served as kitchen chairs and extra seating for visitors. Our scuffed wooden floors and old, cast-off furniture gave the impression to all who entered that this was an unkempt and unclean home.

Because I was only two years old at the time, the word *poor* held no meaning for me, as this was the only life I had known. Winters were frigid, and fuel was rationed as war-ravaged Germany struggled to reestablish its resources. During the winter months, the country's average daily temperature was around 32 degrees Fahrenheit (zero Celsius) or slightly above. We were too poor to afford consistent heat, so our mother tried to keep us warm at night by placing hot bricks wrapped in a towel under the bedcovers by our feet. "I often burned my feet as I slept," Imgard recalled many years later. "I still remember the excruciating pain whenever my feet accidentally got too close to the hot bricks."

The appearance of our home and the poverty in which we lived did not trouble my young mind. My daily focus was on laughing and playing with my sisters and friends until it was time for bed. Having something to eat was never a concern of mine at that point, because when we didn't have enough food on our table—which was quite often—we scurried over to Mrs. Webber's house, where she rescued us from our hunger. We were at her home

Our Flat taken on my trip in 1981

so often we called her "Mutter Webber," as she was more a mother to us than Else was.

On the morning of Wednesday, March 18, 1953, I jumped up from the living room sofa that served as our bed, leaving my two sisters to fight over the covers all three of us shared. I ran to the front window of our apartment, which looked out on the main dirt road running through our village. It was a crisp, cloudy morning, but no rain yet. I smiled, running back toward the sofa. "Wake up! Wake up!" I shouted as I climbed on top of my sisters, tapping my small hands on their heads. "We can play! We can play!"

I ate my breakfast in a hurry so that I could go outside and play before the possibility of rain would force me indoors. Riding my tricycle at breakneck speed down the street, with my sisters and neighborhood playmates, Wolfgang and Helmut, chasing me on their bicycles, was the highlight of the day. The boys were hot on the back wheels of my trike, racing to see who would arrive at the church lawn first. Even at two years of age, my competitive nature revealed itself in play.

We played most of the morning outside, but by lunchtime, having had only bread and tea for breakfast, our tummies growled with hunger. Else sat us down at the table for a meager lunch.

"Finish your sandwiches and milk, girls," Else ordered, "and then you may go to Mrs. Webber's to play with Wolfgang." Imgard and I stuffed our mouths with the thin sandwiches and gulped our milk, then slammed our cups on the wooden table and ran out the front door in anticipation of the fun we were going to have that afternoon. Mother Webber often allowed us to play down the street on the soft, plush green lawn of the church. We scurried toward her house, squealing with delight as we crossed the dirt road with Else in close pursuit.

We entered the Webbers' kitchen. "How are my girls?" Mother Webber shouted happily as she stretched her arms out toward us. We rushed straight into her arms, and she gave each of us a warm, loving bear hug and a quick peck on each cheek. Breaking away from her arms, we hurried to hug Hannelore, Mother Webber's teenage daughter, and Toni, Hannelore's friend. The two girls often helped babysit us since we were there so often. Excited and full of energy, Imgard and I began chasing each other around the kitchen table, never noticing that Helga, our sister, was not there to join in the chase. Helga had been left at home while Else ensured our arrival and chatted briefly with Mother Webber.

"I've missed you. Where have you been?" Mother Webber asked as Else entered the kitchen.

"We've been pretty busy. Times are hard for me. I've been looking for a job, but so far none have come up. Jobs are hard to find, especially here and in the nearby villages," Else explained.

"Yes, we are in hard times," Mother Webber affirmed. "I wish I could help you more, but things are difficult for all of us right now. You know Hannelore and I can take care of the girls whenever you need us to do so."

"I'll keep that in mind," my mother said. "I have to go now, as I left Helga at home by herself."

Before opening the kitchen door, Else turned toward Mother Webber and looked directly at her as she said in a firm voice, "Be sure to remind Gertrud to take the girls down to the church to play, since I can't go myself. I'm staying home with Helga, so I need her help. Thanks."

Else turned and left. Imgard and I stopped playing briefly to watch her exit the kitchen. Little did we know it would be the last time we would see our mother.

Soon Mother Webber's daughter-in-law, Gertrud, and Gertrud's son, Wolfgang, arrived. The little boy, about two years old like me, was elated, squealing with delight as he climbed out of the stroller and ran to join in the fun. The three of us yelled and screamed, chasing each other around the kitchen table with renewed energy. Accustomed to the noise, the adults visited with each other, not protesting when we took our play outside.

Eventually, Gertrud called to us, "Wolfgang, Imgard, Ute, it's nap time." We all scurried into the kitchen. Gertrud lifted Wolfgang into her arms, giving him a hug and a kiss on each cheek before whispering to him, "Nap time, little one. Grandmother will tuck you in."

Gertrud turned toward Imgard and me. "Let's go for a walk down to the church. You can play on the grass for a little while before I take you home for your nap," she said with excitement in her voice. "Both of you hold my hand as we walk, girls. Imgard, you take my left hand and Ute my right."

Gertrud turned toward Mother Webber. "Else asked me to take them to the church to play," she said. "There is someone who is picking them up to take them for a ride. I'll be back soon."

"Who is this person? Does Else know them?" Mother Webber asked with suspicion in her voice.

"I assume she does, as she was the one who made the arrangements," Gertrud said. "I'm helping Else out. That is all she told me. I'm sure it's going to be fine."

The three of us stepped out into the darkening day.

* * *

The road leading from the highway to the Kinderheim was unpaved and, in many sections, much like a roller-coaster ride. Its deep dips and curves swayed Imgard and me from left to right in the black Cadillac's backseat as we passed through several villages along the way. The driver, Mrs. Grammer, was forced to stop every fifteen minutes to let my sister out of the car to vomit.

"Little Imgard had an upset stomach, so I was forced to stop every fifteen minutes," Mrs. Grammer wrote, describing the circumstances under which she drove us to the orphanage. "Imgard's panic and dry heaves delayed what should have been a two-hour trip into a three-hour one."

How helpless and desperate my sister must have felt as she held on to me tightly for the three-hour journey to our new dwelling place. Once we arrived, she clung to me, holding me tightly as we entered the intake office of the Kinderheim St. Josef in Mannheim, Germany.

"The two children were so dirty," Mrs. Grammer wrote. "Imgard's hair was stringy and dirty . . . There was little of her natural blondeness showing through. You would never have known she had blonde hair . . . Their clothes were so dirty I cannot describe them." While the nuns quickly scooped us up to give us a bath and clean clothes, the orphanage's heavy doors slammed shut, locking us away forever from all that was familiar to us.

The Kinderheim's halls echoed with the sounds of

playful laughter, squeals of excitement, and cries from small children and babies who couldn't communicate their fear and loneliness in any other way. Upon our arrival, Imgard clung to me, not letting me out of her sight. She became my "mother," watching my every move, protecting me from anything that she considered dangerous or that might take me away from her. I, too, clung to my big sister, nestling my head on her chest while she wrapped her arms tightly around me in a grip that sent a message to all others: *"We're together. I'm not letting her go."*

How quickly my life had changed. Several hours before, I had been riding my tricycle on the road in front of my home, playing under the watchful eye of my mother, who stood observing us as we passed by the front window of our flat. What had I done that had caused me to end up here among total strangers, with just the clothes on my back and a small, tattered cloth duffel bag that held several of my broken wooden toys? I clutched the bag tightly, as it was the one possession connecting me to the life that had so quickly and shockingly vanished. Gripping my duffel bag between my shaking thighs, I clung to my sister with a grasp that would have been difficult for any human being to undo.

My two-year-old mind racing, I began to ask myself, *Why am I here?* Knowing no answer, I began at that early age to doubt my self-worth, developing feelings of guilt as I continued running through questions that popped into my little mind. *What did I do? Is Mother*

Me at 2 ½ years old

angry with me? Where is my mother? Where is Helga? I want to go home." At the time, Imgard and I were both too young to realize that our own mother was the orchestrator of this horrendous deed.

A significant number of white German mothers abandoned their biracial children, resulting in the establishment and designation of approximately 640 Kinderheims (orphanages) in the 1950s to accommodate the biracial children being given up for adoption throughout the country. Both Catholic and Protestant churches owned the Kinderheims, with hundreds of nuns working and living on the premises. Else had relinquished all her parental rights and released us to the state to be raised in the Kinderheim until we either were adopted or reached adulthood.

Unanswered questions about our whereabouts filled the air and soon spawned rumors among those who knew us. Else had kept the secret of our plight from almost everyone except Gertrud, who had taken us to the churchyard for our fateful ride. Gertrud knew that we were going away but was not sure why or where.

One day, Mother Webber caught her breath as she watched the day's news on television. A short segment on the local news featured several children who were living in Germany's Kinderheims, ready to be adopted. Mother Webber called out to Hannelore, "Look! Come look!" They both stopped still as they saw a picture of Imgard and me with the caption "Ready to be adopted." The news story focused

Advertisement for my Adoption

on the numerous biracial "occupation children" who had been given up for adoption by their German mothers. The government was using television to advertise those who were eligible for adoption.

Mrs. Grammer's picture appeared in the background as the news anchor began to explain the "Brown Baby Project." Speechless, Mother Webber and Hannelore listened intently to the news commentator urging those interested in adoption to contact the Kinderheims directly. This news story aired throughout Europe as the German government ramped up its campaign to recruit couples open to adopting biracial children. It was no longer a secret. All the villagers knew what my mother, Else, had done. We would never return to Mother Webber's loving arms, the village, or the life we had known.

Shortly after the news story aired, Else rose early to make sure Helga was up and ready to go to Mother Webber's house to eat breakfast and walk to school with Hannelore. Else had a long day ahead of her as she prepared herself for the long commute to work in Frankfurt.

"Hurry and get dressed, Helga," Else shouted. "I'm going to be late for work, and you're going to be late for school." When Helga was ready, Else took her hand and walked her across the street to deliver her to Mother Webber's care.

"What time will you pick me up, Mother?" Helga asked, as she did daily.

"I'm working late tonight but will get you as soon as I can," Else replied.

She gave Helga a quick kiss on the cheek, then waved good-bye to her eight-year-old daughter. Mother Webber,

Hannelore, and Helga carried on their daily routine, with the two girls attending school, then returning home to do homework, eat, and play together. Anticipating Else's return from work, Mother Webber gathered Helga's things and stacked them in a neat pile by the front door. They waited and waited, well into the night. Eventually, Mother Webber realized Else wouldn't be coming that evening.

"Time for bed," she told both girls. "Your mother probably had to work late, Helga. You'll see her tomorrow morning or after school," she said in a reassuring voice.

Everyone was optimistic that Else would return, as she always had done. After all, Mother Webber had babysat Helga for several years before my sister and I were born. Else had always picked her up after work, and this time would be no different, Helga's young mind rationalized. Helga rushed to Mother Webber's after school the following day, excited to see her mother.

"Is my mother at home? Where is my mother?" she asked. "Do you know when she is coming to pick me up?"

Else never returned to pick up her daughter after work that day, or the next day, or any day after that. No one heard from Else for years. All who witnessed this genuinely grieved for the little eight-year-old girl who had been suddenly, without warning, abandoned by her mother. Their hearts spilled over with sadness as they witnessed Helga's loss of her two sisters and now the abandonment by our mother. Helga's entire family structure had vanished within weeks, without any explanation. She was alone now, with only the Webbers to rescue her from the fate of being placed in a Kinderheim far from the people she loved.

Although the Webbers never adopted Helga, she was blessed by Mother Webber's kindness and love as Mr. and Mrs. Webber raised her as their own daughter, despite having six boys and a girl of their own to support. Helga became in effect their second daughter, resulting in a sisterly relationship between her and their only daughter, Hannelore. This very close relationship continues to this day.

Else's decision to abandon all three of her daughters in such a cruel and harsh manner has left indelible scars that remain as open sores, either consciously or subconsciously, in all three of our minds forever. No one ever imagined during that time that suddenly being "kidnapped" or whisked away unexpectedly and being abandoned by one's mother would have such lasting effects on a child.

Else gave no warm, loving kiss good-bye. No motherly embrace; not even an explanation. She wordlessly and abruptly walked away once again, shedding her old life for a new one, just as she had done with her firstborn son, Ernst, a decade earlier. Overwhelmed with her life, she was desperate to leave behind her encumbrances and start over as a single woman without her three little girls.

Half-Sister Helga, me - Ute,
Sister Imgard - 1950

CHAPTER VI

THE BROWN BABY PROJECT

"It takes a village to raise a child."
—African proverb

It was a common perception among Germans that "brown babies" would be better off being adopted in their fathers' countries, or at least sent to live in nations that had large black populations. Not only white Germans but also African Americans believed that mixed-race German children were better off living among "their own people," even though the children were German citizens, spoke the German language, and knew no other country.

These views appeared in African American newspapers in the United States and a few German newspapers, such as the conservative nationalists' newspaper *Bild-Zeitung* and the Mannheim-based *Abendpost*. Open debates, articles, and research data, along with discussions both private and public, ensued as to the biracial child's ability to succeed academically and socially in German society.

With race being a robust issue at the time, both the American and German governments concluded that adoption was the fastest and most efficient way of resolving the enormous biracial baby "problem" spawned by World War II. Both governments worked collaboratively to match "brown babies" to African American military families stationed in Germany and throughout Europe, and to send them to African American families living in the United States. This partnership tapped adoption as the most convenient solution to what every war brings: mixed-race children who were not accepted by their birth country nor their fathers' country, and were repeatedly abandoned by both parents.

Most of these orphaned children went to the United States, while others remained in Germany to be adopted by other Europeans in such countries as Denmark, Sweden, and the Netherlands. Biracial German children were caught in the middle of the racial upheaval in Germany and the United States. My sister and I were no exception to this all-too-common theme of racism and segregation once my mother signed her "Irrevocable Statement of Consent," allowing the German government to determine our destiny.

The first two Afro-German "brown babies," a boy five and a girl six years of age, arrived in the United States to meet their adoptive parents on October 4, 1951. Their adoption was by proxy, meaning the children never saw their adoptive parents before arriving in the United States. They were the first of many adoptions, including my own, conducted by Mrs. Mabel Treadwell Grammer and her Brown Baby Project. She was a journalist and civil rights activist who strongly believed in Germany's declaration that the "brown babies" would be better off being raised by "their own kind."

Mabel Treadwell was one of seven children born to a bellhop father and a stay-at-home mother in Hot Springs,

Arkansas, in 1914. She graduated with a degree in journalism from the University of Ohio. After graduation, Mabel began writing for the *Baltimore Afro-American* newspaper, more commonly called the *Afro*, where she was a mover and shaker who battled discrimination and segregation throughout her life. She fought the War Department and won, becoming instrumental in desegregating Arlington National Cemetery.

In 1950, Mabel married army Chief Warrant Officer Oscar George Grammer Sr. Being stationed in Germany, she had time on her hands to visit the German orphanages. She fell hopelessly in love with the beautiful "brown babies" who were filling up the German orphanages but were not being adopted by other Germans because of their brown skin and mixed race. Unable to have children of their own, Mabel and Oscar began adopting biracial children from orphanages throughout Germany while they lived in Karlsruhe, Mannheim, and Stuttgart.

Nuns working in the Kinderheims would often ask Mabel, "Is there any way you can take one more?" Determined to save as many "brown babies" as possible during her time in Germany, she could not resist saying yes. Mabel and Oscar first adopted a ten-year-old boy, which began their odyssey of adopting twelve biracial German orphaned children, whom they took back to the United States at the end of Oscar's tour of duty in Germany.

Mrs. Grammer witnessed the struggle of white German women who had biracial children by soldiers stationed in Germany during the war. Recognizing the dilemma many of the mothers were facing, she made it her mission to save as many children as possible by pioneering her very own personal campaign to set up adoptions for these children.

"I have always been a hater of organizations and red tape, so I decided to work fast while I could to help other families before some organization decided to tie up these children for the rest of their lives," she wrote in a letter to my new mother dated June 22, 1953. She also expressed her belief that the Kinderheims were "cold, heartless" places for children to live.

Her strong passion for saving children gave Mabel a laser focus on placing biracial children in homes across Europe as well as in African American families, both military and civilian, living in the United States. She worked closely with African American families Stateside to coordinate the tedious adoption process to its completion.

In the 1950s, most of the adoption process was done solely by mail. Mabel did not use the help of the German social services but relied on her own personal contacts to get the word out to potential parents. She had many volunteers, including military families, friends in the United States and in the German village in which she lived, and the nuns at Kinderheim St. Josef in Mannheim, who helped process the necessary paperwork to place the children for adoption in homes throughout Europe and the United States.

She could not have done this enormous task alone. The old African proverb "It takes a village to raise a child" certainly applied to Mrs. Grammer's efforts to secure adoptive homes for

Baltimore Afro-American Newspaper

abandoned and lost biracial German children with more than 500 willing couples. She rallied an entire community who were of like mind and focused on a common cause, including Sister Oberline, Hans Proksch, many staffers at the *Baltimore Afro-American*, and numerous people employed by agencies that were pertinent to Germany's adoption process. They worked together tirelessly to save as many abandoned biracial children as possible, connecting them with parents throughout Europe and the United States.

Without Sister Oberline, the sister superior who ran Kinderheim St. Josef, where my sister and I had been placed, Mabel's Brown Baby Project would never have taken hold there. The nuns and Mabel worked closely together to get us ready both physically and mentally for our new life with our adoptive parents. In a letter to my potential adoptive parents, Mrs. Grammer explained that often adoptees arrived at the Kinderheims "dirty, hungry, simply neglected," either due to poverty or because their mothers no longer wanted them. Imgard and I were no exception to these circumstances.

Sister Oberline recognized the need to move the Brown Baby Project forward and often escorted the children to the Frankfurt airport, releasing them to the custody of the airlines. In November 1953, she escorted her last group of "brown babies" headed to America, as the closing of the German visa quota would be at the end of the month. Her last known assignment was in service to the Kinderheim in Friedberg, Germany, after having served Mrs. Grammer's Brown Baby Project at Kinderheim St. Josef for more than three years.

Another nun who was instrumental in volunteering her services was Sister Mella. She was featured in the May 1953 monthly *Afro* newspaper accompanying a group of children to the Rheim-Main Airport and signing forms releasing them to Scandinavian Airlines to begin their journey to a foreign country where they would meet for the first time their new adoptive parents. The Guiding Angel was the name given her as she poured her heart and soul into the project, accompanying the children to the US Consulate, where they were given a final physical examination ensuring they were in good health to make the seventeen-hour plane ride to the United States. After the completion of their physicals, Sister Mella escorted them to the airport. Eventually diagnosed with a grave heart condition, Sister Mella was transferred to the Kinderheim in Friedberg, where she joined Sister Oberline for the duration of their service in the Catholic Church.

Another crucial member of Mabel's team was Hans Proksch, a very capable Scandinavian Airlines employee who pulled strings in Frankfurt and in Stockholm, Sweden, to obtain transportation at reduced rates for the German-American children to come to America. He worked closely with Mabel and the *Baltimore Afro-American* to cut airfares by fifty percent, making the tickets affordable for more adoptive American parents. The airlines also agreed not to require the new parents to pay for having a flight attendant accompany the children on the flight. Each group of "brown babies" was provided food, beverages, and tender care during the long flight to America. Proksch processed all Brown Baby Project airline tickets efficiently and promptly, ensuring that the children safely reached their destinations.

With the many volunteers in place, Mabel Grammer began a very focused marketing campaign by writing articles about the "brown babies' " plight in the Kinderheims and frequently including their pictures. Mabel's articles were also published in the popular German newspaper *Bild-Zeitung*, which helped to spread the Brown Baby adoption information throughout Europe. My sister and I, along with hundreds of other children, had our pictures published, advertising our availability for adoption. It was a very effective way of reaching thousands of African Americans who might be interested in adopting a biracial German child. With hundreds of children readily available for adoption, Mrs. Grammer's focused marketing campaign caught the attention of many couples throughout Europe and the United States.

One person who read Mrs. Grammer's articles in the *Baltimore Afro-American* was Marie Harriette Ellis-Fambrough. Having had numerous miscarriages and desperately wanting to start a family, she responded to the article by writing a letter of inquiry on January 24, 1953, expressing her interest in adopting a child through the Brown Baby Project. Mrs. Grammer had heard about two biracial little girls living in squalor with their mother in the village of Bingenheim. Rumor had it that we might be good candidates for her adoption project. Mabel quickly followed through, validating the rumors by arranging an introductory meeting with Else at our home sometime in January. Upon receipt of Marie's letter of adoption inquiry, Mabel decided that we would be a good match with the Fambroughs.

A month later, on February 20, 1953, Mrs. Grammer responded to Mrs. Fambrough's inquiry, describing my sister and me as perfect candidates to consider for adoption, in an appeal to Marie's heart to say yes to the match:

The little girls were living with their mother, who

had little food. They were cold, living in filth and dirt. Imgard's hair was stringy and dirty, so much so that there was little of her natural blondeness showing through. You would never have known she had blonde hair until it was thoroughly washed. Ute's was the same. Their clothes were so dirty I cannot describe them . . . When I think of the condition of these poor little girls, filthy and in sickness, I know that all they needed was love and care.

After witnessing our plight, Mabel returned to Bingenheim to try to convince Else to give Imgard and me up for adoption. During the visit, Mrs. Grammer took the opportunity to observe our personalities. "Ute is a small happy child, always laughing, always in the mood for fun," she wrote in a letter to the Fambroughs, "while Imgard is a quiet sad child. She knows her mother didn't love her."

Mrs. Grammer returned to meet with Else several times after our placement in the Kinderheim on March 18, 1953. The purpose of her visits was to acquire as much family history as she could, such as birth dates, ages, and any medical information Else could provide. Mabel also talked extensively to Else about the adoption and what would be required from her to complete the process. Mrs. Grammer quickly notified our American parents that she had crossed a significant hurdle in convincing Else that we would be better off being adopted by people in the United States who could afford to clothe and feed us.

Else knew Earl was permanently gone. He had walked away from the relationship after having discovered her in bed with the neighbor. Under pressure from Mrs. Grammer and knowing that she would no longer receive financial support from Earl, nor the monthly care packages his mother had sent from the United States, Else chose to give us up. Anxious to have the business completed, she signed an Irrevocable Statement of Consent witnessed by a notary public, releasing us to the Kinderheim for adoption.

Mrs. Grammer wanted to make sure our potential American parents realized that Imgard and I were a "package deal." Explaining why it was so crucial for the well-being of both of us to be adopted together, she wrote in a letter to my adoptive parents,

> Their mother held out a long time before signing the papers releasing them to the Kinderheim. Their mother does not want them separated. She . . . wanted to make sure they went to a good home for a better life. Imgard has always had a great fear that she and Ute will be separated and when someone at the Kinderheim takes Ute, she immediately starts crying. When she is assured they will always be together she stops crying but takes her sister's hand and tries to hide her in a closet or cupboard. She has a loving attitude and fought off any attempts at . . . friendliness and cried when she thought she was losing Ute.

It was soon discovered that Else's signature was not the only one needed to place Imgard up for adoption. A technicality on Imgard's birth certificate temporarily halted our release to America. It was discovered that Else had not been officially divorced from Ferdinand Schaab when Imgard was born. Although they had long gone their separate ways, the courts had not finalized the divorce. At the time of Imgard's birth,

Else listed Ferdinand Schaab as the father instead of Earl, naming her "Imgard Schaab" on the birth certificate. This single but significant action by Else gave Ferdinand parental rights and joint legal custody of Imgard. His signature was needed along with Else's to begin the adoption process. Without his consent, my sister Imgard could not be adopted. A full review of both our birth certificates revealed that Else was legally divorced by the time I was born, so my surname was Claassen, Else's maiden name.

Mrs. Grammer took matters into her own hands in order to expedite our trip to America and clear any other hurdles that might hinder our adoption in the United States. She drove the document to the Veteran's Hospital in Bad Homburg where Ferdinand had been committed and explained to him the situation. He willingly signed the Irrevocable Statement of Consent, releasing his parental rights and opening the door for Imgard and me to be adopted together.

Once both parents had signed the release papers, Mrs. Grammer went to the Kinderheim to visit my sister and me twice daily in hopes we would adjust to our strange new surroundings and forget our mother. Feeling comfortable that the adoption would happen, she authorized the sisters at the Kinderheim to begin telling us about our new parents in the United States before we took the long flight to America the following month.

Critics of her efforts pointed out that Mabel did not do background checks or meet with adoptive parents beforehand, but conducted most of her matchmaking through the mail. They also pointed out that there were no home visits, no inspections, and no personal counseling sessions provided, as an adoption agency is required to do. Mrs. Grammer fought back, maintaining that if Germany was unable to guarantee the equal treatment of the "brown babies," she had every right to make it her mission to seek loving homes for them. Soon her critics desisted as they witnessed her passion and love for her Brown Baby Project. They saw that she worked tirelessly to give each child the opportunity for a better life.

Mable Grammer, Joe & Marie Fambrough
(Daddy & Mama)- 1956

CHAPTER VII

NEW BEGINNINGS

"Give the ones you love wings to fly, roots to come back
and reasons to stay."
—Dalai Lama

The night was cold and moonless. Showers pelted our bright yellow raincoats as Imgard and I entered the Frankfurt International Airport to take the redeye flight to New York International Airport, or Idlewild, as it was commonly known then, on May 9, 1953. My sister and I were with three other "brown baby" rescues from the Kinderheim boarding the plane to meet our American adoptive parents. Sister Mella had taken care of us at the

My Flight Bag and Toys to America

Kinderheim and earlier that day had accompanied all of us to the US Consulate to get our physicals before releasing us to the custody of the Scandinavian Airlines flight attendant Jean Cole. Jean was assigned to attend to our needs during the seventeen-hour flight and to ensure that we were released to our new parents waiting for us in America.

Preparing for the big trip was a happy and exciting time for Mrs. Grammer and my soon-to-be mother, Marie. They collaborated together through numerous letters, going over every meticulous detail of what was needed for the long trip to America. Mrs. Grammer measured Imgard's and my body and head sizes using thin strips of paper as measuring tapes. She then mailed the measuring pieces to America. Marie could barely contain her excitement as she shopped for her two little girls. It was important to both Marie and Mrs. Grammer that our new American clothes fit. After all, we weren't just going on a plane ride; we were beginning a new life in a new country with a new family. This historic, life-altering occasion demanded that we look our best.

Marie shipped the brand-new outfits, underwear, and accessories overseas to the Kinderheim. My sister and I boarded the plane wearing matching outfits: blue corduroy pants, white cotton T-shirts, red double-breasted jackets, shiny white saddle oxford shoes, and knitted caps to complete our snazzy look. We were the best-dressed German "brown babies" on the plane. We had never worn clothes of the latest fashion, in such bright, vibrant colors and soft materials.

Headed to America–Me in Sister Melba's arms

Seventeen hours and numerous time-zone changes later, we landed on the runway in Queens on May 10 to begin our new life. Joe and Marie Fambrough (Daddy and Mama) had flown from Bakersfield, California, to New York the day before to await our arrival.

"We hardly slept," Daddy said with excitement in his voice and grinning from ear to ear whenever he told the story of our arrival in America. "JoAnn [Imgard] was frightened when she first laid eyes on me, but once she saw Marie, she was all right. I knew she feared being in a foreign country speaking no English, which was a huge adjustment to ask a small girl to suddenly make. That's why I stayed my distance from her and focused my attention on you while Marie was attentive to JoAnn," he told me.

Imgard, now called JoAnn, and I, no longer Ute but Judy, spent the night with our new parents in a beautiful New York hotel. Our parents had planned a brief stay in the city so that we could get acquainted with each other before heading home to friends, relatives, and the community of folks who were eagerly awaiting our arrival. The following day, we went on our first family outing, exploring the wonders of New York City.

"JoAnn had a loving attitude toward Judy," Daddy recounted. "When we were shopping in New York, she would glance back instinctively from time to time to make sure Judy was still there." My sister continued to keep a close and cautious eye on me, assuring herself with every glance my way that we were still together. Separation at this crucial time, when we had just recently been abandoned by our mother, would have been devastating to both of us.

We stayed several days in New York, getting more comfortable with our new parents and adjusting to America with all its noises, smells, and tastes that we were experiencing for the very first time. Daddy wrote in his letter to Mrs.

Grammer describing how he was acclimating us to our new country, "We introduced them to a variety of American food and treats on our day outing in the city. Judy loves fruit and ice cream while JoAnn had her first taste of watermelon. She loves watermelon and hot dogs." After our adventure in New York, we flew to Los Angeles, and from there Daddy drove the two hours to our new home in Bakersfield, California.

Bakersfield, located in south-central California, has a unique and colorful history. In 1863, Colonel Thomas Baker claimed the swamplands along the Kern River, where he built his home. Because of his generosity and hospitality, his home soon was known as "Baker's Field," which became a stopover for travelers entering the San Joaquin Valley searching for a new life. Little did we know we were headed to a small town whose history was deeply rooted in southern norms, values, traditions, and customs, resulting in blatant racism and discrimination that earned Bakersfield the nickname "California's Deep South."

The town's southern roots run deep within the people who migrated there from Arkansas, Louisiana, Missouri, Oklahoma, South Carolina, and Texas shortly after the Civil War had ended. Remaining sympathetic to the Confederate cause, they migrated to Bakersfield, Kern County, in the hope of finding jobs to support their families. Southern whites found work in the very lucrative and productive oil fields in nearby Taft. The oil fields during this time employed only whites, while southern blacks were hired to work in the backbreaking cotton fields or fill a rare custodial job.

Bakersfield has a hot desert climate with long, hot, dry summers and short, cool, slightly moist winters. The long summers make the region suitable for growing cotton and a variety of other crops, such as carrots, citrus, almonds, and pistachios. Commercial cotton farmers began recruiting southern blacks to work in their hugely profitable cotton fields, eliminating the reliance on Chinese labor. By 1884, more than 1,500 southern blacks had relocated to Bakersfield, bringing their transferrable field-working skills with them as they toiled brutal hours for little pay picking cotton under the blazing sun.

As the cotton bolls mature and open, exposing the locks of cotton, it dries, and cotton burrs make the chore very painful for the hands and fingers. The fields are also full of cockle burrs, which are painful when handled. Worms that gorge themselves on cotton leaves are another hazard, a pest with an agonizing sting. The work of a cotton picker stretched patience and tolerance to the limits.

Although California entered the Union as a free, non-slavery state in 1849, framers of the state constitution wrote into law the systematic denial of civil rights to nonwhites, who were refused the right to vote, own property, and intermarry, among many other restrictions. With southern roots deeply embedded in Bakersfield's culture, the Ku Klux Klan easily established a local chapter in 1921, spreading its influence throughout Bakersfield and Kern County. As is well documented, many of its members were prominent government officials who worked for many years in the mayor's office, police department, sheriff's department, and judgeships, as city school district board members, and on the county board of supervisors. Respected community members by day and hooded terrorists by night, they beat, lynched, and committed arson, driving out anyone—black, white, or brown—who opposed them.

In the early 20th century, the African American population still had very few civil rights. Bakersfield restaurants refused to serve everyone who entered, unapologetically posting signs outside their establishments declaring "No Niggers or Okies." Oildale, a neighboring town, became infamous for its billboard warning sign "Niggers, Don't Let the Sun Set on You," boldly posted along the bridge that once connected Bakersfield and Oildale. As late as 1975, thirteen black athletes were run out of the neighboring city of Taft by a white mob angry because they were dating white girls.

Attempting to become an independent businessman and buy a home in an all-white neighborhood became quite the challenge, as Joe and Marie Fambrough experienced firsthand, encountering the wrath of the Bakersfield Ku Klux Klan.

My adoptive father, Jawayne Fambrough, known by everyone as Joe, was a self-made man. Born in Los Angeles in 1912, he moved to Bakersfield after his mother's death from cancer. With only the clothes on his back and seventy dollars in his pocket, he was determined at age seventeen to become financially independent. Aware of the Ku Klux Klan's activities, he kept a low profile, focusing on earning an honest living and determined to one day establish himself as a successful entrepreneur.

Joe was hired as a janitor at the local drugstore in the old Haberfeld Building on Chester Avenue shortly after his arrival in the city. Soon after he got the job, his younger brother and sister also moved to Bakersfield, seeking a new life away from the trappings a big city like Los Angeles offered. Joe knew he needed to increase his income to help support them until they gained financial independence. He was pleased that they were all together to help each other grieve over the recent death of their mother.

White real estate businessmen frequently boasted about their accomplishments as they waited patiently in the lobby of the Haberfeld Building for the elevator to open its doors and carry them up to their designated office floors. Daddy listened intently, catching bits of their conversations as they talked about their business deals. "I knew I wanted to be successful like them and real estate was the way to earn lots of money," Daddy told me with pride in his voice. "Naturally it takes money to make money, so I opened a savings account at Bank of America. I saved almost every penny I made. With every paycheck, I would go directly to the bank and deposit money into my savings account, even if it was just a few cents. Every penny adds up to be a dollar," he said.

At the age of twenty-one, he became an entrepreneur, establishing Imperial Floor Service, which installed, finished, and refurbished hardwood floors throughout Kern County. Determined never to be poor again, he continued to save his money faithfully, never forgetting the white businessmen in the Haberfeld Building who were profiting from the many real estate deals they were making. Eventually, Daddy would fulfill his dreams by becoming a self-made millionaire. By the time of his death, he had acquired fifty-three pieces of property and a hotel on the coast, while having streets named after him in the housing tracts he funded and developed: Fambrough Drive in Bakersfield and Fambrough Street in Santa Clarita, California.

Working long, hard hours and saving every penny he

could, Joe reached his savings goal; he set aside enough money to pay cash for a house that would be his first investment property. However, no realtor, property owner, bank, or escrow company would do business with a black man. Determined not to let racial prejudice and discrimination get in his way, he quickly circumvented the system by finding Wayne Vaughn, a successful white Bakersfield businessman who was sympathetic to his plight. Until the racial property ownership barrier was lifted, Vaughn bought real estate property with Daddy's money. After escrow closed, Vaughn would issue a quitclaim deed transferring the title and property into Daddy's name. Their business arrangement resulted in a lifelong business partnership and friendship.

* * *

Joe married Marie Harriette Ellis on April 13, 1938. Marie was born in Oklahoma in 1912 and ventured to Bakersfield with her family as a child. She graduated from Bakersfield High School and many years later graduated with an AA degree from Bakersfield Community College. She was a licensed beautician and known in the community as a civil rights leader and activist, being honored nationally for her work on women's rights issues during the time she was president of the Women's Political Study Club. She held several appointed positions, serving on the Bakersfield Fair Employment Commission and the Republican Central Committee. Realizing their values were not the same as those of the Republican Party, Marie and Joe switched and registered as Democrats during the Kennedy-versus-Nixon presidential election. Upon the early establishment of the Imperial Floor Service, she served both as office manager and bookkeeper until Imgard's and my arrival in America. Both

Joe and Marie were life members of the National Association for the Advancement of Colored People (NAACP).

Daddy worked hard at his Imperial Floor Service business, diligently saving for their dream home, which they bought in an all-white neighborhood on Second Street before our arrival. Daddy was talented and blessed with a green thumb. The beautifully landscaped yard often found him on his knees pulling weeds from the lush, green dichondra lawn or planting beautiful roses of every color imaginable. The immaculately kept yard was often the talk of the neighborhood. Many who stopped over to visit while he was out working in the yard sought Daddy's gardening advice. Maintaining a neat, landscaped yard was very important to him, as he was determined not to give his white neighbors a legitimate excuse to sell their homes and move. In the wee hours one morning, still embraced by darkness, Daddy was awakened by the snapping and crackling sounds of fire. Sprinting into the living room, where the large French provincial bay windows faced the street, he came face-to-face with a burning cross on the front lawn. More irate than afraid of the message the burning cross was sending to those who saw it, he quickly recovered and began to shout orders.

"Marie, call the police! Marie, call the fire department first, then the police!" as he sprinted out the front door. Turning on the outdoor faucet and grabbing the garden hose, he sprang into action with the sole purpose of minimizing any further destruction. Everyone was safe, but the KKK message rang loud and clear throughout the all-white neighborhood, and especially throughout the African American community.

One by one, the white neighbors began moving out after

realizing Daddy would not give in to the hateful bigotry of the
KKK. Three of his direct neighbors decided to flee the now-
integrated neighborhood by putting their homes up for sale.
The house to the right, the house to the left, and the house
directly behind posted "For Sale" signs on their front lawns.
Just as quickly as they were posted, Daddy bought the houses
and sold them to African American couples who shared the
same values and desired the lifestyle the neighborhood had
to offer. "White flight" gave Daddy the opportunity to invest
heavily in real estate, buying these properties and selling
them to couples who were running into difficulties acquiring
a bank loan because of the color of their skin. Integrating
the neighborhood was his contribution to the civil rights
movement—quietly opening the door of opportunity for those
who suffered racial discrimination in good old Bakersfield.

Having settled into their new home, Joe and Marie
struggled to get their family started. After several painful
miscarriages, Marie became despondent and lost hope in their
dreams of having a family to make their lives complete. One
day while reading the *Baltimore Afro-American* newspaper,
she became intrigued by Mabel Grammer's article about the
plight of the occupation babies who were living in orphanages
throughout Germany. After talking it over with Joe, Marie
wrote a letter to Mrs. Grammer stating their willingness and
readiness to adopt a child from Germany. After getting to know
them through correspondence, Mrs. Grammer convinced Joe
and Marie to adopt Imgard and me, keeping us together. There
was no doubt in Mabel's mind that Joe and Marie would be
loving, caring parents who could financially support us. Mrs.
Grammer was confident of the latter point after reviewing
supporting documents submitted to establish their claim of

having the means to support my sister and me until adulthood. Mrs. Grammer and the Fambroughs worked closely together to ensure that the path toward our adoption would be smooth.

When my sister and I arrived at our new home in Bakersfield, I gazed in wonderment at my new surroundings. I'd never seen such green grass or so many beautiful flowers as we drove up to the bright white stucco house with its deep, rich green trim that stood out among the other homes in the neighborhood. We had never seen such a beautiful house before. The outside was pristinely cared for. Not one noticeable blotch stood out on the white stucco of its exterior. Along the driveway grew hybrid roses of every color: red, yellow, white, pink, and orange, extending along the full concrete path leading to the detached garage. The yard was a testament to Joe's "green thumb" and his love of gardening.

Even though there was a buzz in the community about the Fambroughs' adoption of two biracial German orphan girls, the fanfare was minimal upon our arrival in Bakersfield on May 13, 1953. No ticker-tape parade or balloons to greet us. No adoption or welcome-home party, no friends, no family of any sort to shout, "Welcome home!" as we entered the house.

Daddy wanted a quiet arrival to our new home, without the hoopla. He believed we would be overwhelmed by the noise, the strange faces, and the language barrier. There was a need to

New Beginnings-Daddy, me, Mama, Joann

establish trust between our new parents and us, especially in light of Imgard's frightening memories of the physical abuse she'd experienced at the hands of our mother, which remained fresh and vivid in her mind.

Our new parents hoped that interaction with other children our ages would ease the pain of the past. Shortly after our arrival, Mama and Daddy took us next door to meet their good friends Mr. and Mrs. Mangrum. We were blessed to have such a great family living next door, as we became instant friends with their children, Lorraine, Michael, and Elaine Mangrum. We were all about the same age.

"We played jacks, hopscotch, mud pies, and hide and seek," Elaine told me as she reminisced about our childhood years together. "How we all managed to communicate, I don't remember. However, children seem to have a universal language when it comes to playing together. We became fast friends, and the fondness we felt for each other transcended the language walls."

As more and more African Americans began buying homes, creating a diverse community, Second Street grew to be a close-knit neighborhood with parents and their children developing lifelong friendships with many families: the Fords, Edwardses, Mangrums, Suttons, Johnsons, Marichinis, Williamses, Keys, Marions, Hopkinses, Henrys, Lions, Ginns, Youngs, Whitfields, and Strongs, as well as Lawrence Fambrough, who was Daddy's brother and my Uncle Buddy. As neighbors, relatives, and friends, we all enjoyed numerous get-togethers, such as potluck meals and holiday celebrations. Many of us as children attended our neighborhood schools together, and some of us belonged to the same church.

May was a perfect time for us to arrive in the United States, especially for JoAnn, who was turning six the following month, on June 29. She was just the right age to enter first grade on September 9, 1953, at Wayside Elementary School.

"JoAnn is quite a little lady," Mama wrote to Mrs. Grammer. "She is brilliant. She is really excited to start attending school in September, as she is speaking pretty good English. We are hiring a tutor to prepare her for school." I joined in JoAnn's tutoring sessions, which Mama decided to conduct herself. The tutoring became a daily mother-and-daughter bonding session drawing all three of us closer together.

JoAnn's first birthday in America arrived, and the air was filled with excitement. This new environment with new parents would be one to remember, as kindness in her life was long overdue. Mama dressed JoAnn in a brand-new white lace birthday dress similar to the ones often worn for Catholic children's christenings. JoAnn's olive complexion and straight blonde hair neatly braided in two pigtails gave her an angelic look as she bent to blow out all six of her candles. A halo around her head was the only thing missing. She was too much of a little lady to squeal with excitement, but she did break out in a wide grin as she quickly crossed the dining room floor to straddle her brand-new red bicycle. The adjustment was going well.

As the days, months, and years passed, JoAnn realized the traumatic past was behind her as she began to adjust to her new life in America. She worked hard to learn English and to assimilate into the American way of life. Her first day of school would be the first time she and I would be apart for any length of time. Mama and Daddy were concerned about how the separation might affect us.

In a letter to Mrs. Grammer dated October 21, 1953, Mama wrote, "I've never seen such devotion between two little sisters. When JoAnn returns from school each day, one would think she had been away for weeks. Such a reunion! Judy is such a chatterbox while JoAnn is the perfect little lady."

My first birthday in America was celebrated at my home with neighborhood and Sunday school friends in attendance. At three years old, I beamed as Daddy rolled out my brand-new red tricycle with rubber tires and a shiny silver bell that drove everyone crazy as I enthusiastically rang it over and over again, squealing in delight. Being somewhat of a daredevil and tomboy, I often rode at breakneck speed on our long concrete driveway, which was lined with dozens of plush rosebushes armed with thick, healthy thorns on every branch. I remember clearly the numerous falls, scrapes, and scratches on my legs as I learned with determination to maneuver up and down the path of our driveway, avoiding head-on collisions with the rosebushes.

The subconscious emotional effects of having been abandoned raised their ugly heads as I tried to adjust to my new life in America. The residual trauma manifested itself early on in my wetting the bed and having frequent nightmares. Upon arrival in my new home, I would wake up in the middle of the night to find that my pajamas and bedsheets were soaking wet with urine. My new mother would lay a sheet of plastic under a clean, fresh sheet so I would not ruin the mattress, then tuck me again safely in bed, giving me a peck on my forehead as she left the room. As I reached kindergarten age and could help change the soaking bedsheets, I was embarrassed each time it occurred.

I did not understand why I wet the bed or why I sometimes had nightmares and woke up in the middle of the night so frightened that I climbed into my sister's bed, seeking safety and comfort. The wetting slowly subsided as I became more acclimated to my new surroundings, but the nightmares lasted much longer. Once I began to feel more secure in my new environment, I became better equipped in mastering the art of mind control. My nightmares lessened over time as my mind began to find peace. As maturity set in, I learned to wake myself up from my nightmares, calm myself down, and control the content of my dreams by focusing my thoughts on positive images and memories.

A third emotional effect resulting from Else's abandonment shows itself on rainy days even now, just as it did when I was first trying to adjust to my new life and surroundings. There is a particular smell that comes with the rain that sends me sinking into a state of depression. As the rain begins to fall and the smell fills my nostrils, a thick, dark cloud covers my spirit, and I find myself fighting with all the mental strength I can muster to ward off the inner gloom. My mind at first was too young to understand why, but as I grew older and began to listen to Daddy's "life lessons" on the effects our conscious and subconscious minds can have on us, I reached the conclusion that the depression was not a chemical imbalance in my brain but rather a subconscious memory related to the trauma of being sent away to the Kinderheim.

Having my days filled with schoolwork, playtime, sports,

music, and high expectations from my new parents left me little time in those childhood years to give in to the "down in the dumps" feelings that plagued me then and still do even now. Rainclouds and the smell and sound of rain triggered my subconscious mind to remember an event that my conscious mind has suppressed, even to this day: being abandoned by my birth mother and whisked away from the only life I had ever known.

"It was raining the day Mrs. Grammer picked you girls up," our friend Hannelore told me on my first visit to Germany. "It was a short rain but enough to soak the ground. Several hours after you left, the rain stopped and the sun came out to finish the day."

* * *

Our new American mother was the ultimate model of the 1950s housewife and mother, much like the June Cleaver of that era, or Harriet Nelson of *The Adventures of Ozzie and Harriet,* or Margaret Anderson of *Father Knows Best.* At that time, African American women predominantly held jobs like housekeeping positions and others in the service industry, while white women who worked outside the home did so as nurses and teachers—the nurturing, caregiving professions. Mama held a unique position in our community as an African American woman who didn't work outside the home. Upon our arrival, Mama stopped working to stay home and become a full-time mother and wife.

Mama was the solid foundation of our home in meeting our physical and developmental needs: preparing daily hot, healthy, home-cooked meals, keeping the house clean, and making sure we completed our homework. Every morning she would put on a crisp housedress and comb her hair into a neatly rolled bun. Then she would wrap a stylish apron over her housedress so that no accidents would ruin her clothing while she cooked for us. Mama believed that the most important job she could do was to stay home and be a supportive wife to her husband and mother to her children. Her job was to help raise healthy, well-adjusted children and prepare them to become

Me, Mama, JoAnn - 1953

independent, self-supporting adults. She willingly and quickly slipped into her role and remained in it until her death. Her abiding love and devotion to her children and husband were never questioned.

Many remember fondly how kind, loving, and sweet she was, living her Christian faith daily. Mama modeled the power of communication and leadership through her participation in church services and activities. She wrote and published the church's weekly bulletin, taught Sunday school and summer vacation Bible school, and chaired a variety of church and community events. Her life lessons on love, respect, and being a good, practicing Christian are values she passed on to me.

Mama dressed us in frilly dresses and patent leather shoes with lacy socks. She made sure our teeth were brushed and our hair neatly combed as we prepared to enter God's house of worship for morning and evening services on Sundays, and for Wednesday night Bible study. Mama often told us, "This is God's house. We will show him respect and reverence by being clean, neat, and appropriately dressed." She role-modeled her expectation by being one of the best-dressed ladies in church. Beautiful dresses and tailored suits with matching shoes, purse, gloves, and hat to complete her outfit became her signature appearance at Sunday morning services.

Although JoAnn and I attended Charm and Modeling School, it was in church that we learned the art of being a lady by sitting with our legs crossed at the ankle and hands placed on our laps and listening intently to the sermon. There was no instrumental music at our church, so everyone was expected to sing and know the hymns. Mama often sang and hummed church songs at home so we learned to sing on key and to harmonize together. As I became proficient in reading music and playing the piano, we were able to sing our church songs to music at home.

Shortly after my arrival in America, the civil rights movement began, and would span from 1954 to 1968. Its goal was to secure the same legal rights for African Americans that white Americans enjoyed. On May 17, 1954, the US Supreme Court ruled unanimously in the Kansas landmark decision *Brown v. Board of Education of Topeka* that racial segregation in public schools violated the Fourteenth Amendment of the United States Constitution. This meant that black children could now attend the same schools and learn in the same classrooms as white children. A year later, I began kindergarten at McKinley Elementary School. At four years of age, soon to be five shortly after school started, I was too young to equate the color of one's skin to race and what it meant with regard to attending school in America. I was excited for the opportunity to go to school daily just like my big sister. I knew she would help me assimilate into my educational surroundings.

Education was extremely important to both of my parents. Mama was the gatekeeper and Daddy the enforcer of our academic grades. It was understood with no exceptions that only A or B grades in any of our classes were acceptable. Bringing home a C would not be tolerated, and the offender would meet swift consequences in the form of a spanking. Mama went to Parent Teacher Association (PTA) meetings at every school that I attended. She worked her way up to become president of the McKinley Elementary School PTA and of the Emerson Middle School PTA during my attendance at both schools. At a time when it was widely held that a woman's place was in the home, Mama was out in public, her name known among the community leaders as an education and political activist. I sat among my friends feeling proud of my mother as she spoke clearly, with elegance, and with authority to diverse groups of parents who listened and respected what she was saying.

I had overcome a big challenge in my life, as my bedwetting and nightmares had ceased during my elementary school days. My self-confidence was on the rise. I vaguely remember the good times I had in elementary school. Kindergarten consisted of music, singing, laughter, and getting to know other children. This was my opportunity to interact with a diverse group of children from a variety of areas surrounding my neighborhood. We got along well with each other, unaware until we got older that our skin coloring and gender would make a difference in how we were perceived and what doors of opportunity would open or close to us as we progressed through life.

I felt like I never fit in either racial category that society wanted to place me in so readily as I advanced into my middle school years. JoAnn was my full-blooded sister. We shared DNA from the same biological mother and father, yet we were so different in hair and skin coloring and facial features. Born with fair skin, hazel eyes, and straight blonde hair like our German mother's, JoAnn inherited her facial features from our African American father, Earl. I was born with chocolate brown skin, brown eyes, and a head full of woolly dark brown hair like our father's, but inherited my facial features from Else. Yes, JoAnn and I were full sisters, born from the same parents, but oh how far apart in eye, skin, and hair coloring we were.

Mama and Daddy were very much aware of our uniqueness during the early 1950s, as there were very few biracial couples and fewer biracial children born during this racially charged time. My adoptive parents knew how skin coloring could hold power over a person's perception of another human being and become a stumbling block to achieving one's life goals. Being business owners, community leaders, and social activists, they lived and worked in both worlds, black and white, so they made a conscious effort to pepper our lives with a diverse group of children and adults upon our arrival to America.

Peer pressure and the drama of middle school created a very challenging time for me, as awkwardness, racial identity, and skin coloring took precedence over all other issues. Race and skin coloring were not something I knew or thought much about before middle school. The need to be accepted by my peers was strong during this natural stage of growing up. *Who am I? Where do I fit?* were questions looming constantly within me as I navigated my world. My brown skin identified me as black, but my curly dark brown hair that flowed down my back, long eyelashes, and European facial features kept me from being fully accepted among my peers in the African American community. A common question boldly asked by my peers and even adults of all races, "What are you?" or "What are you mixed with?" was asked on a regular basis and continues to be asked even now.

Two fellow African American female students who singled me out for my looks would often walk behind me, following me partway home from school as they taunted me. "You ain't black!" they shouted. "You think you're better than us 'cuz of your long hair and you talk white. You're nothing! You just tryin' to be white!" They yelled their accusations in genuine hate and anger.

The experience was frightening, but like so many other students who are bullied mercilessly, I didn't say a word to anyone. I was determined to deal with it alone, employing a variety of strategies to avoid running into them on my way home. Although the image of those two female students remains vivid in my mind even now, I have chosen not to publicly identify them. Many years later, I was the classroom teacher to the child of one of them, but I never spoke of the subject when she visited my classroom on the evening of Back to School Night. I have forgiven but not forgotten those two tormentors.

Relief from the bullies came when Mama enrolled me in the school music program. It gave me the opportunity to develop friendships with students from a variety of different cultures. No one questioned my long hair or asked what I was. We were all there focused on a common purpose: to make beautiful classical music for others to enjoy and to make our parents proud of our accomplishments. This involvement led me to become a member of the Emerson School Orchestra and the Bakersfield City Schools Honor Orchestra.

The Emerson School Orchestra performed regularly at school and community events. My cello was too heavy to carry home, so Mama picked me up daily from school, which, to my relief, eliminated the two girls' opportunity to bully me. My self-esteem grew as I became more proficient with the cello and no longer had to worry about the bullying. Recognizing my natural musical ability, Mama hired a private piano instructor who gave me weekly home lessons. My musical accomplishments were a start toward the development of positive self-esteem.

Daddy and Mama began very early in my life providing me with the tools necessary to navigate skillfully in the two worlds in which we lived. They both recognized the value of learning the norms of both the African American and Caucasian cultures. We frequently attended community events that provided us the opportunity to learn the standard or pattern of social behavior that is typical or expected from each respective group. Taking cello and piano lessons, attending plays and classical community concerts, and enrolling in J.C. Penney's Charm and Modeling School gave me the opportunity to learn the norms, values, and customs of white American culture at an early age.

At the same time, being raised by African American parents, JoAnn and I attended numerous family functions and family reunions, and Daddy's direct approach to making sure we understood the norms of black America was with us daily. Growing up in an African American church, attending NAACP community events, serving as youth president of the NAACP, and being a participating member of the Student Nonviolent Coordinating Committee (SNCC) during the civil rights era helped me become familiar with the values and customs of black America.

In order for any minority, especially African American, to become successful, it was essential to develop the survival skills necessary to navigate Bakersfield's racist norms and culture. Family, school, and social events became my training ground as my parents worked diligently to teach me the art of code switching: acting or talking more like those around you, a necessary skill to acquire to be successful living in both worlds. Race and code switching were a significant factor in our lives, and code switching allowed me to be accepted for the moment by those at whichever culture-sponsored event I was attending. Living in an integrated neighborhood, going to family reunions, and attending a predominantly white church in Oildale during my teenage years allowed me to practice my code-switching skills in order to prosper in high school and in the world around me.

Daddy decided I would receive a better, more focused education by attending Garces Memorial High School, a small, private Catholic school nestled in an all-white community off Panorama Drive. Ready for a positive change from my middle school bullying experience, I rationalized that my school life would attract much less drama in a high school of 500 students than in a school of 3,000. And in fact, it did turn out to be the best choice for my educational goals.

I was one of the first five African American students

accepted to attend Garces Memorial in the fall of 1964 with 500 white students. Transportation was not provided, nor were scholarships given during this time to assist those who could not afford to pay the tuition and buy the textbooks and school uniforms needed to attend this prestigious school. Because it was located miles away from my neighborhood, I rode the city bus, making a transfer at Vest Drug Store on Chester Avenue in downtown

Garces Memorial High School Cheerleader–1967

Bakersfield. Rain or shine, I walked the five blocks daily to the neighborhood bus stop to catch the hour-long ride to my high school up on the hill.

Riding the city bus daily gave me time to think about my career goals and visualize my future. Becoming a teacher, giving back to my community, helping others, and becoming a financially independent woman were the goals I had established for myself. Education became a priority in order to accomplish them. I was reminded daily of the plight that faced uneducated black women, as many domestic workers rode the city bus headed to the white neighborhoods where they cooked, scrubbed, and cleaned homes in the Panorama Hills. Although it was honorable work, it was a reminder that without education, the doors of opportunity for a black woman were minimal. It also validated the many talks Daddy gave me on getting a good high school and college education. "Once you have a good education, no one can take that away from you. Education is the key to living a financially independent life. You don't have to depend on anyone," Daddy would tell me during one of his many "teachable moment" lectures.

Attending Garces Memorial High School with students who were born into some of the most prestigious and successful families in Bakersfield gave me the opportunity to see firsthand what could be acquired through education and hard work. I was excited and enamored by the beautiful, large, custom-built homes that surrounded the school. My parents often reminded me that my roots were grounded in our own neighborhood, but my educational opportunities were there at the school.

Daddy liked to give me lectures and demonstrations of life lessons that I refer to as "teachable moments." One day I accompanied him to the Bank of America then located on Chester Avenue and Third Street to make a deposit, as he'd just closed escrow on one of his investment properties. I knew being invited to accompany him meant he had a teachable moment in store for me. Before entering the front doors of the bank, he turned to me and said with a big grin on his face, "I have one million dollars in cash deposited in this bank. Just you watch and see how much power there is in having money." No sooner did we enter the bank than a white gentleman in a business suit approached us, greeting my father by name as he extended his hand.

"Hello, Joe. Good to see you today. How can I help you?"

Daddy handed him an escrow check, undoubtedly no small sum, and the man immediately escorted us to the bank elevators and rode with us to the top floor of the building. The elevator doors opened directly into the bank president's office. I thought I was in the movies, as I had never seen such a beautiful office filled with dark oak furniture so shiny with wax you could see the reflection of your face. Large-pane glass windows overlooking the city surrounded the office. Daddy confidently strode toward the president, shaking his hand firmly as he looked directly into his eyes, making the symbolic statement "We are equal as men." I watched as they walked over to two plush dark-brown leather chairs, where they conducted their business while I stood a discreet distance away.

Upon leaving the bank, Daddy explained to me, "Now that I am a successful businessman with a considerable amount of money deposited in their bank, they treat me with respect. I'm not just a black man to them but also a man with a million dollars cash deposited in their bank. All they want is to figure out how to get their hands on my money. They want to negotiate my real estate investment loans in ways that make them more profitable, but I have news for them. The only color they see is green.

"Always remember: Money talks," he summed up in a matter-of-fact tone as he unlocked the doors of his El Camino truck.

I often reflect on that experience and how Daddy, an African American male with an eighth-grade education, overcame all the obstacles to become a successful businessman. The odds were stacked against him, with his mother dying, and his moving to Bakersfield at seventeen years old and taking on the additional responsibility of caring for his younger siblings upon their arrival shortly afterward. Having graduated from the school of hard knocks and determination, Daddy was a man who refused to let anything get in the way of accomplishing his goals and dreams. He knew that formal education for my generation was the key to financial success, and he was passing his words of wisdom on to me every chance he got.

Daddy was a proud, stubborn, and determined black man. He steadfastly refused to use the "Colored Only" restrooms and drinking fountains that permeated Bakersfield. When Mother Nature called, he would take the long drive home to use the restroom, get a cool drink to refresh him, and then return to continue his business for the day. No one was going to make him feel "less than," which was a powerful lesson for me to witness and learn.

Realizing the devastating subconscious effects that racism, prejudice, and discrimination had on anyone's self-esteem and self-worth, Daddy kept one of the first copper wire tape recorders along with headsets that he placed on the nightstand by his bedside. Every night he would turn it on, put on his earphones, and then lie down to listen to positive affirmations being spoken as he fell asleep. Yes, he was way ahead of his time. He wrote positive affirmations daily, keeping them tucked in his shirt pocket right over his left breast, ready to be pulled out to reflect on throughout his day. "Don't ever use the words 'I can't'! You can become anything you want if you set your mind to it!" he instructed in an authoritarian voice, pointing his finger at me with a stern look on his face. It was a direct order with no tolerance for rebuttal.

Daddy and Mama taught me life lessons that provided me with the tools necessary to navigate between both the black and white worlds in which we lived. Wealth and status in the community allowed him to function smoothly in both worlds, whether he was socializing or conducting business. His talks, lectures, and teachable moments often centered on education, civil rights, code switching, and living with hardworking Christian values. I am grateful for the gift they gave me, helping me become a successful, educated, independent woman.

CHAPTER VIII

MY SEARCH AND DISCOVERY

"Family is not defined by our genes . . . it is built and maintained through love."
—*Momatlast.com*

It is common for those who were abandoned by their parents to experience the strong feeling of "not enough" that well up to drown our self-worth and self-esteem. No matter the circumstances, there is a powerful sense of rejection and abandonment when a birth parent, especially our mother, relinquishes all parental rights and walks away from us, never to be heard from again. Only when we meet the challenge of finding the answers to the many questions spinning in our heads do we conquer our fears and reach a positive state of self-awareness.

My search was driven by my desire at a very young age to know my biological history, to discover all aspects of myself, and to answer the question *Who am I?* I felt the answer was the cause of my bedwetting and nightmares, the root of my deep depression during rainy weather, and the key to my self-discovery. I was reminded how little I knew about myself every time I went to the doctor and had no answers to the usual battery of questions about my family health history.

I remember distinctly when one of my sixth-grade English assignments was to write a paper describing my parents and determining which one I looked more like. I wrote about my adoption and pledged to meet both of my biological parents face-to-face one day as they willingly answered all my questions: *Why did my mother give me away? What ever happened to our sister Helga, who remained in Germany? Whom do I look like? Whose personality did I inherit? What genetic traits did I inherit from my parents? Who were my grandparents? Did my mother truly love me?*

I didn't know much about my biological parents, as my only information was that given to me by my adoptive father. Daddy's version was clear, concise, and consistent every time he told the story: "Your mother loved you very much. She wanted you to have a better life, so she gave you up for adoption, because we could provide a better life for you here in America." He would often pause, then wrap his arms around me and continue in a soft, compassionate voice, "We chose you, so that makes you very special and very much loved."

Although I knew Daddy and Mama loved me, I questioned the validity of the reason why I was given up for adoption. Something deep inside of me knew there was much more to my story, and I was resolute to discover the truth firsthand, rather than rely on someone else's account of what happened and why.

Call it arrogance, but I knew one day I would travel to Germany to meet my biological mother, visit the village where my childhood began, meet any villagers who might still remember me, and, last but certainly not least, visit the orphanage where I lived until I was adopted and brought to America. I was going to get the answers to all my questions by conducting my own interview with my birth mother, never thinking of the logistics involved, or the consequences the interview might have for my sisters and me. The bonus for me was to identify any genetic biological similarities as my mother willingly and truthfully answered all my questions. Then and only then would I feel satisfied that I had discovered the truth as told to me by my birth mother. I never considered the possibility that she would refuse to answer my questions, or the unthinkable: that she would refuse to acknowledge my very existence.

I also knew for certain that I would one day discover, find, and meet my biological father. Although he was certainly on my mind during my life, tracking him down was secondary to finding my mother. Besides, there was a different set of questions for him: *Are you my real father? Did you love me? Did you love my mother? Why didn't you marry her? How could you have allowed her to give us up for adoption? Where were you when we were whisked off to the Kinderheim in the middle of the day? Did you ever try to find us?*

Because my birth father was a soldier in the United States Army, I knew he had less control over his life than my mother did in many ways. Call it sexism, but for me, my focus was on my mother, whose very existence I had relied on to sustain me. She was the one I had depended on, from conception until the day she sent me off to the Kinderheim. Yet I felt sure that one day I would find both of my birth parents.

Life happened as I continued on with my education, graduating from high school, attending college, marrying, and having children; yet the search for my biological parents always remained in the back of my mind. A few weeks after turning eighteen, I gave birth to my firstborn, a son, Christopher Aaron Billingsley. As the nurse placed him in my arms, a surge of love and total devotion overcame me as I pledged to be the best mother possible, providing for and protecting him with all the power and strength God had given me. My son would not acquire any abandonment issues from me. Through trial and error, he and I would see it through until he became a responsible, independent adult.

Although I had become a mother, Daddy felt I was still much too young to be given my adoption papers. "You'll have to wait until you are older and more mature before I give them to you," he told me as I pressed him for more information. His statement gave me a ray of hope that in the future I would eventually receive those papers. Once that day arrived, my search would begin.

Five years later I gave birth to another son, Chad Michael Billingsley. I pledged once again to be the best mother possible as a surge of love and total devotion once again overcame me. One day in 1977 while visiting my parents, I again raised the topic of receiving my adoption papers.

"Daddy," I said, "I'm married now and the mother of two sons. Don't you think it's time to give me my adoption papers?"

"Well, I don't know," he hedged. "What are you going to do with them once I give them to you?

"I'm going to read through them, hoping I can find the answers to some of the questions I have. Besides, I've always told you I wanted to meet my biological parents at least once."

Daddy left the family room and returned with a small ladder.

"I've got something for you, Judy," he said, glancing at me with a glimmer in his eyes as he carried the stepladder into the kitchen. Placing the ladder on the floor, he took a few steps up, positioning himself directly under one of the ceiling panels. He lifted the white panel with his left hand, and his right hand disappeared into the darkness above.

Out from this hiding place, he retrieved a large cardboard shoebox. My mouth opened, but no words would come out as Daddy carried it down the ladder and walked over to me with a wide grin. Stretching out his arms, he handed me the box.

"I think you're ready now," he said. "Since you're married and have children, you're mature enough to handle its contents."

He was pleased that he had surprised me as he saw the look of shock on my face. I laid my sleeping son down on the couch and wrapped my arms around my father in a bear hug.

"Daddy, Daddy! Thank you so much!" I burst out. "You don't know how much this means to me!"

"I'm not sure how much Marie will appreciate me giving this to you," he mused. "She's a bit nervous about you searching for your birth parents."

"But, Daddy," I said, "you know that both of you will always be my parents no matter what. You guys raised me, and I love both of you so much. You will always be my parents."

"I know, but she isn't feeling that way."

"Then I'll tell her when she gets home. I'll assure her that she has no need to be concerned."

My intended search had just become much easier, as I had been handed the very tools needed to accomplish that goal: my adoption information. Daddy had just given me the keys to my roots. But Mama's attitude worried me. She was feeling betrayed, and nothing I said that day put her fears aside.

I carried the dusty shoebox with tender loving care, gently placing it on the floor behind the driver's seat of my car as if it was made of crystal and might break at the slightest movement. Driving home with my heart pounding, I contemplated what pertinent information the shoebox might hold for me. Would it contain the names, addresses, and phone numbers of my birth parents? How many papers were there? Could I read them, or would I need to hire someone to translate all the documents written in German? How useful would any of the documents in the shoebox be to me in my search for my biological parents?

Later in the evening, with my boys tucked in bed sound asleep and my husband snoring in our bed, I gently carried my precious shoebox into the family room. I took the lid off, bubbling with excitement as its contents came into view. There, lying in a six-inch stack of neatly folded papers, was the key to the mystery of my beginnings. As I carefully began emptying the box, I discovered a variety of letters, newspaper clippings, legal documents both in German and in English, and German Christmas cards. As I pulled each paper out of the shoebox, I organized them into piles separated by subject. I was anxious to read each one thoroughly in search of any clues that might move me closer to discovery.

My primary focus was on determining whether any of the papers held the full names of my biological parents. Looking at the numerous piles of folded legal papers, letters, and court documents, I unfolded a small, card-size paper written in German. It was a copy of my birth certificate. Knowing that a birth certificate is essential in identifying parental lineage and validating one's very existence, I squealed with delight in anticipation of its long-held secret.

Quickly, I scanned the document for the German words *Mutter* and *Vater*. There, right before my eyes, was the name of my biological mother staring back at me. Yes, at last she was no longer a mystery but a person with a name, a full name: Else née Claassen Schaab. I stared at her name, then glanced at my birth date to assure myself that I had been celebrating the correct one all those years.

My excitement grew as my eyes quickly scanned down to the line marked "*Vater*" to discover the name of my biological father. To my utter dismay, "unknown" was written on the line. I was horrified. Questions quickly ran through my mind: *Why wasn't his name written? Did my mother, Else, truly not know who my father was?* But, reminding myself that this was just the beginning of my research, I felt hopeful that his name would appear among the numerous documents I still needed to read.

It took several days to pore through the translated documents and letters thoroughly, as each was written in German and then translated into English as a second document. Among the many papers, Earl Laughton from Norfolk, Virginia, was named as biological father to both my sister and me. I was elated. Because he'd served in the US Army and his last known address had been in the United States, he would be the easier parent to find, especially since we spoke the same language and lived in the same country.

I never doubted my ability to find my biological parents, even during a time when the only readily available technology was the Xerox machine, the electric typewriter, and the single-line home telephone system that provided directory assistance as part of its customer service support. Improvements to the telephone system were made over the years, as customers relied on directory assistance to provide them with specific phone numbers or addresses. This was especially necessary when looking for the telephone numbers of those living out of state. Dialing 411 gave you access to a directory assistant who could provide you with the home phone number and address of a requested residence, business, or government entity. With this, you could reach just about anyone in the United States.

I immediately dialed information and was told that the area code for Norfolk was 757. I then dialed 411 and asked directory assistance for the phone numbers of any Laughtons listed there. Although many Laughtons I spoke with told me I had the wrong number, I wasn't discouraged. Working through my list, I finally hit the jackpot when an elderly woman answered the phone in a shaky "Hello."

"Hello, ma'am," I said. "I have been researching my family tree and saw the name Earl Laughton listed as a possible relative of mine. I wanted to talk with him to find out if we are related. Do you know him?"

"Why, yes, honey. That's my son," she responded with eagerness in her voice.

"I'd like to speak with him to get further information on my ancestry, ma'am. Do you have his phone number?" I asked in a calm voice, not wanting to reveal my excitement.

"Just a minute. Let me grab my telephone book."

I could hear her moving about as she reached for her handwritten telephone book. I could picture in my mind her thick, crumbling old personal address book where family and friends' telephone numbers were written, with many crossed out and changed for those who had moved.

After a moment of rustling through papers, she said, "Here it is, honey," and read off the phone number of my biological father. I repeated the number back to her slowly, making sure I had written it accurately. "Oh, thank you so much, ma'am," I said, trying to contain my excitement and nervousness at the same time.

I talked with her for a few more minutes, asking factual questions I knew any mother would have the answer to. "Was your son in the army? Did he serve in Germany during World War II?" She was very forthcoming as she told me he was married with four children and now lived in Pemberton, New Jersey. He was still serving his country, stationed at Fort Dix Army Base.

My heart was pounding as I hung up the phone and considered my next move. What was I going to say? How would I know I had the right person? What if he rejected me and denied that I was his daughter? What would I say and do if he did reject me? And how would I let him know that I wasn't out to tear his family apart?

I knew that whatever the outcome, I had to try. I had to give it my all, even though his rejection would hurt me deeply. I could not let this moment go by, as I might not have the nerve to do it if I put it off till later.

I picked up the receiver again and dialed the number his mother had given me. Knowing that my father's wife or one of his children might answer the phone, I was ready with my "official business" tone when a small child's voice answered.

"Hello," I said. "May I speak to Mr. Earl Laughton, please?"

"Just one minute. Daddy!" I heard. "Someone is on the telephone for you."

Waiting for him to come to the phone seemed like an eternity. I pinched myself to make sure I wasn't dreaming. With my stomach turning over and a lump in my throat, I quickly searched for the first words I would say to my biological father, Earl.

"Hello?" The voice was friendly.

"Hello, Mr. Laughton?" I said in my best professional tone.

"Yes. Who's this speaking?"

"I am researching my family tree and came across your name," I said. "I am not sure if this Earl is you, but I have been calling all the Laughtons listed to determine if we are related in any way. Did you ever serve in the United States Army in Germany during World War II?" I forced my voice to sound natural and steady.

"Yes."

"Were you stationed in Frankfurt, Germany?"

"Yes, I was," he said. I could hear the smile in his voice.

"Did you ever live in a German village off base at times?"

"Yes."

I hesitated but knew I had to complete my mission. Would he man up?

"Well, I think I'm your daughter."

There was silence.

I wasn't sure what to expect. Was he going to accept my existence or deny it? Would he hang up the phone, never to be heard from again? Would he reject me? Deny me? The oxygen went out of the room around me as I sat on the edge of my chair, not sure what would come next.

He hesitated, laughed nervously, then asked, "What is your birth date?"

"October 1, 1950." Silence ensued.

"Well, yes, you're my daughter," Earl said. He sounded happy.

Relief entered my body as a big smile spread across my lips. *He acknowledged me! I am real to him!* I let out a big sigh, then hesitated for a moment, knowing that my mission would not be complete without including my sister in this conversation.

"Well, I think you have another one," I told him as I, too, laughed nervously. "I have a sister named JoAnn."

He laughed again and asked me, "What is her birth date?"

"June 29, 1947," I answered.

"Yes, she's mine, too," he said.

My heart was full of joy. I had discovered a part of my roots. We talked briefly, exchanging telephone numbers and giving each other a few quick details about our current lives. Earl stated that his current German wife was aware of his relationship with Else and knew of our existence. I appreciated his openness and honesty, and assured him that I was not contacting him to interfere in his current life or seek any monetary gain. Up front and out in the open was and always has been my mode of operation.

After my conversation with Earl, I immediately called my sister JoAnn. "I found him!" I yelled into the telephone before she could complete her hello. Stunned, she was speechless, which allowed me to fill the silence with my jabbering as I described in detail my search strategy to locate him, my phone conversation with his mother (our grandmother), and my conversation with Earl, as well as my next steps to continue open dialogue with him in hopes of meeting him face-to-face one day.

* * *

Although Daddy expressed his approval of my search, Mama was very much opposed to my efforts. There was no convincing her that my effort to find my birth parents was not a betrayal of her status as my mother. Guilt and betrayal are two emotions that are common stumbling blocks for many adoptees who search for their birth parents. Reading my adoption papers and occasionally communicating with Earl was all that I was willing to do until Mama either gave her approval or had passed away. Mama died on February 12, 1981.

After her death, Earl and I communicated more frequently. Feeling comfortable that I would place no unreasonable emotional demands on him or his family, Earl and his wife invited me to visit them in New Jersey. At thirty-one, I was finally going to meet my biological father, whom I had no memory of. It was a "mission: impossible" assignment that had finally come true.

The day of meeting Earl and his family arrived in the summer of 1981. Landing at Philadelphia International Airport, I acquired a rental car for the hour-long drive to Earl's home in Pemberton, New Jersey. As I drove, I rehearsed what I would say upon first meeting him face-to-face. JoAnn had arrived several days earlier and was waiting along with Earl and his family for my arrival. Earl had a beautiful split-level home with a large American flag waving gently in the breeze from a tall flagpole cemented firmly in the ground. I rang the doorbell. In a moment, there stood Earl with a warm, welcoming smile as he opened the glass storm door.

Not knowing what to do, I shook his hand, mumbling, "Hello, pleased to finally meet you."

He shook my hand and welcomed me into his home. JoAnn swiftly came from behind him to greet me with a warm bear hug as I entered the living room.

"Glad you made it," she said with a big grin.

Earl quickly introduced me to his German wife and their daughter and three sons. As I shook each one's hand, I was overwhelmed with how quickly my family tree had grown. I now had additional biracial, half-German brothers and a sister who were now a part of my extended family.

The next morning I woke up to discover JoAnn alone, reading silently in the dining room.

"Good morning," she said as we gave each other a hug.

"Where is everyone?" I asked.

She shrugged her shoulders. "Earl is at work, but I'm not sure where everyone else is. This is how it's been each morning since I got here."

Seeing the kitchen clean, with no food preparation evident, not even coffee, I said, "I guess we are on our own. I'll take a shower and get dressed, then we can go get breakfast." We quickly realized that our rental car would be put to good use.

Having our own transportation was essential to having the freedom to explore while Earl was at work. It also became a necessity, as it was our only means of acquiring a meal other than dinner. We vowed not to make waves but rather to go with the flow and simply drive ourselves to a variety of breakfast and lunch spots while exploring the New Jersey countryside. Although there was some interaction with the Laughton sons, we seldom saw Earl's wife and daughter, as they were often in another part of the house enjoying each other's company.

Retirement was quite a few years away for Earl. He worked as a mechanic on the army base, leaving early in the morning before JoAnn and I were awake and returning just before dinner. His work schedule allowed us to interact with him only during the evenings upon his return home. He had the difficult task of trying to navigate between our needs and those of his wife and children. Seeing him struggle and feeling the tension in their home mount with each passing day, we moved up the date of our departure. We had no desire to cause anxiety within the Laughton home.

Once we'd informed Earl of our decision to cut our visit short and return home early, he promptly got out several large photo albums and placed them on the kitchen table, gesturing for us to sit down in the seats next to him. There in front of me was what I had been searching for all my life: validation that I had been born. I truly existed at ages younger than two. As he turned each page, I gasped as I saw several of my baby pictures staring back at me through the plastic covering that protected the old photos glued to the album.

Was I really once a baby? Although I knew the answer was yes, an important piece of my life was missing from my memory, and there had been no documentation available to fill in the gaps in my memory of early childhood.

A significant portion of my life had been missing, and I felt it whenever my peers showed their baby pictures and spoke of their early childhood experiences. I had never seen a picture of myself as a baby or toddler in Germany. Seeing my baby pictures in the "Else and Baby Ute" album provided me with the evidence I had known must exist but had needed so much to witness.

For the first time, I saw a photo of my biological mother, Else. She no longer was a figment of my imagination but a real, live human being who had a nose, a mouth, eyes, hair, and skin coloring that made her real. Else, my mother, was brought to life in that moment forever, validating that I had been born and not hatched! Earl began to explain each one of the pictures that documented his life with us in Germany.

Else and Me/Ute–1950

Before JoAnn and I left the next morning, Earl promised to send us copies of the pictures. Six months later, he telephoned.

"Judy, I've found your mother, Else; your babysitter, Mother Webber; and Hannelore, her daughter. They are all alive, living in Germany."

I became ecstatic but couldn't believe my ears. "My mother is alive? My babysitter in the village is alive?" I shouted for joy.

"Yes," Earl responded. "Do you have paper and pencil?"

"Yes, wait. Yes!" I shouted.

Earl had opened the door to discovering my German roots. It was the boost I needed to answer the question *Who am I?* This meant one day soon I would visit the village where I was born, meet the people who remembered me, and visit the orphanage where my sister and I lived until we were adopted and brought to America. All my questions about my adoption would be answered. A giant step had just been taken toward answering many of the questions I had pondered throughout my life.

Not letting too much time pass, I went to the library to do my research about Germany and the German language. During this time, computers, the Internet, and personal cell phones were not yet available to the average person. Finding German translators and interpreters could prove to be difficult, but my job as a high school teacher allowed me access to the bilingual skills of one of my fellow educators who taught German at the same school. Writing to my babysitter, Mother Webber, in German with this teacher's kind help paved the way for communicating with my German family. With little more than paper, pen, envelope, and several stamps, the international boundaries gradually opened. I began to plan a return trip to Germany. It was the journey of a lifetime: the discovery of me.

CHAPTER IX

RETURNING HOME

"Each of us feels the wounds of homeland
deep in his heart."
—*Victor Hugo*

In 1986, five years after meeting Earl, I flew to Frankfurt, Germany, to explore my roots and to meet my birth mother face-to-face. Else née Claassen Schaab had agreed to meet with JoAnn and me to answer our questions. It was the motivating factor in my taking the seventeen-hour flight back home to my place of birth. JoAnn decided to join me in Germany, as she also had many questions that needed answering.

I had tracked down my older sister, Helga, who was very much alive and well, living in Friedberg, Germany, as a single parent raising two daughters, Daniela and Britta. Our babysitter, Mother Webber, her husband, and their adult children were well also, and eager to get reacquainted with us now that we had resurfaced. Although the Webbers' sons and daughter had moved to nearby towns and villages, Mr. and Mrs. Webber remained in Bingenheim, living in the same house across the street from the flat where we had lived until our departure.

Arriving in Germany was a lifelong dream come true, as my goal of discovering my roots and seeking the answers to my many questions was coming to fruition. I had no emotions to quell, no apprehension, because I had no memory of my German life. This allowed me to focus on my personal research with little emotional distraction. It was a far different scenario for my sister, who had unpleasant flashbacks that gnawed at her conscious mind more often than she would have liked.

After JoAnn and I gathered our suitcases upon arrival at the Frankfurt airport, Helmut, Helga's boyfriend at the time, directed us to the car. Helga and Imgard held hands as they walked in the airport parking lot, gazing into each other's face, searching for long-lost childhood memories. Since neither spoke each other's language, Helmut, Daniela, and Britta were our interpreters.

Our weeklong visit was filled with thrilling moments. After a forty-five-minute drive from the airport, we arrived in our home village of Bingenheim to find it thriving and rife with memories of the past. At Mother Webber's home, her six sons and only daughter, Hannelore, were awaiting our arrival. As we got out of the car, Mother Webber, with tears streaming down her face, hugged JoAnn and me as if we were her own long-lost children. She had been not just our babysitter but our support socially, mentally, and physically, often feeding us when we had no food of our own to eat. She was devastated when she discovered that Else had given us up for adoption. Now, after thirty-three years, Mother Webber's "little girls" were standing right in front of her, all grown up.

There were many tears, much laughter, and an abundance to talk about. Although the older generation of Germans didn't speak English, Mother Webber's adult children and Helga's daughter spoke enough English for all of us to communicate. Walking out the front door of the Webber home put us on the street where we had laughed and played so many years ago. The Webbers described in detail the dingy, gray apartment where we had lived with our mother and, at times, Earl. As we stood there, many of the older villagers who had lived through World War II rushed out of their homes, shouting our German names, "Ute! Imgard!" as they raced with arms outstretched to embrace us. They spoke quickly with excitement as they began to reminisce in their native tongue about our childhood and what they knew.

A surge of pride and a sense of belonging swept through me as I heard my German name being shouted out by numerous people. Just as the baby pictures Earl had eventually sent me validated my childhood existence, the old men and women of the village authenticated my connection to this place. I belonged here. I was home. Although my memory was blank, the villagers had not forgotten me. I mattered to them, even if I didn't matter to our mother Else.

The main purpose of my visit was to meet with my biological mother face-to-face, with the agreement that we could ask questions about her and our life in Germany. Now married, with two sons, Reinhard, age 29, and Jürgen, age 27, she faced the dilemma of exposure, as she had never told her husband or family about our existence. Else intended to slip away from them to see us at Hannelore's apartment in Frankfurt. Else's secret was held by many who didn't find it necessary to ruin her new life by exposing her deepest, most personal secrets to her spouse.

Else had agreed to meet with us despite her deeply held secret. But I was unaware at the time that Helga had coerced her into the meeting by threatening to expose our existence to her husband if she didn't meet with us. The evening before our meeting, Helga, JoAnn, and I met to brainstorm and write down all our questions to ask Else. After an emotionally exhausting night stirring up the many questions we had held for a lifetime, we were prepared for tomorrow's extremely important meeting.

Sitting on the patio, Helga and JoAnn reminisced about our time in Germany as a family. Unpleasant memories came to the fore as they talked about the fateful day JoAnn and I were picked up and driven to the Kinderheim while Helga was locked in the bedroom closet.

"When you saw me through the window, I was crying because I didn't understand why Else made me stay in the house and wouldn't let me go outside to play with you. I knew something was wrong when she grabbed me by my collar, dragged me away from the front window, and locked me in the bedroom closet," Helga recounted in a sad voice. Her memory of the fateful afternoon would never grow dim, but would haunt her for the remainder of her life.

Else had locked Helga in the closet for what seemed to her an eternity. As an eight-year-old girl, she was confused and distressed. Why didn't her mother come to let her out? Surely Else heard her cries of fear as she stood banging on the thick wooden closet door, calling out, "Mutter!' Mutter! Let me out, Mutter!"

Relief and assurance that all was well didn't come— not for a long time. Helga dropped to the dusty wooden floor, where she sat feeling defeated and exhausted from her screeching cries. She grew thirsty and chilled. Finally, she yanked one of her mother's dresses down off its hanger and wrapped it around herself, finding some comfort in its warmth and the smell of her mother's perfume as she lay on the floor. Sleep was the only respite from the wild imaginings flooding her mind as to what could be happening outside her cramped, smelly enclosure. *Where are my sisters, Imgard? Ute? Where is Mutter? Will you ever come back? Oh, please come back . .* Helga thought as she drifted off to sleep.

"I waited for hours. Then finally Else came and opened the closet door," she said, reaching for a tissue to wipe away the tears. "I sensed that you were gone but wasn't sure whether you were outside or across the street at Mother Webber's house. I began shouting your names, Imgard! Ute! as I frantically searched for you, looking under the bed, under the couch, and in the backyard. I raced across the street to Mother Webber's house and demanded to know where you were."

By the time Helga was released from the closet, we were many miles away from our home. Else told her that we had gone to live in another village far away. Eight-year-old Helga, with tears streaming down her face, realized what our mother had done. Not aware of Else's next move, and fearful she might be next, Helga continued to live her daily routine with her mother and the villagers, but was plagued by uncertainty about her own fate.

Tears of hurt, anger, and rejection flowed as Helga and JoAnn shared their flashback memories. It was a daunting and very emotional experience for them, and for me to watch. This was the opportunity for Helga to brief us on her life in Germany after we'd left. She recounted how Else had abandoned her shortly thereafter. As time went on, Mother Webber discovered where Else was living but never told Helga, keeping silent as she continued to raise her as her own. It was only when Mother Webber began helping Helga to make wedding plans that she suggested Else and her husband receive a wedding invitation. After Else attended Helga's wedding, she returned periodically to visit the Webbers in Bingenheim, bringing along her husband and their two sons.

The morning of our meeting with Else, the three of us, Helga, JoAnn, and I, headed to Frankfurt, where Hannelore and our mother were waiting for our arrival. Hannelore greeted each of us with a smile and a warm hug as she welcomed us into her home. Guiding us toward a gentleman seated in one of her living room chairs, she introduced us to our interpreter, who was a professor at the Goethe University Frankfurt. We had hired an interpreter who had no vested interest or bias, regardless of the direction the conversation might go. His sole purpose was to interpret accurately both in German and in English what was said during our meeting.

Seated on the couch was a short, stocky, blonde, older-looking woman who got up and extended her hand for us to shake. I searched her face for something that might trigger my memory, but to no avail. Else wore a red, sleeveless nylon blouse, a printed skirt that picked up the red in the blouse, and black flat sandals. Her blonde hair was cut short with bangs, and a tapered close shave at the base of her neck. Her hair coloring and hairstyle were similar to Helga's and JoAnn's.

As she returned to the couch, a scowl appeared on her face, and she crossed her arms as if to protect herself from the barrage of questions she anticipated would be coming soon. There was no warmth, but rather a hard, unsmiling person sitting in front of us, clearly wishing she could have been any place other than right here with the three daughters she had abandoned decades earlier.

When asked about our adoption, Else responded by defending her decision, explaining that she had lost several jobs when her employers found out she had biracial children. She was destitute and needed money to support us. When Mabel Grammer came along offering a better life for Imgard and me, Else took her up on the offer, releasing her parental rights to the Kinderheim. Although that seemed like a valid excuse for us, Else never satisfied Helga's question as to why she was abandoned to be raised by the Webbers. A heated argument in German followed between Helga and Else which the interpreter didn't bother to interpret, and we didn't ask him to do so.

As we returned to the car, I leaned back, resting my head on the seat back and closing my eyes as I focused on quieting my mind to center my emotions. A deep sadness blanketed my body as I realized how difficult the session had been, especially for my sisters. I myself could detach emotionally, as I simply didn't remember anything. For them, the session conjured up more anger and pain, reopening wounds that were never going to heal in one session. The result was that Else returned to her life just as we returned to ours, still broken and with little comfort that anything had been resolved, forgiven, or healed.

My heart was heavy as I flew home the next day to the United States. But there was little time to digest this deep and painful emotional experience. Life—motherhood, work, and community responsibilities—needed my full attention. My career was on the upswing, as earning a bachelor of arts degree and California Secondary Teaching Credential afforded me the income and stability every family wants and needs.

I became a single parent raising two sons. They were my priority, and I focused on being their support as they made their way through life's challenges. High school graduation, college life, military enlistment, and family vacations all took priority over my lingering desire to continue seeking the truth about my adoption.

Retiring in 2008 provided me the opportunity to immerse myself full-time back into the search for the truth about my birth mother and my adoption. Having raised two successful young men who became husbands to successful women and fathers to my four beautiful grandsons, I returned to the voice calling to me, *You're not finished yet. Dig a little deeper for the real truth.* With time on my hands, I had no excuse not to do my "homework," searching every avenue until I had satisfied my curiosity and answered all my questions. I would return to my German roots not only to visit but also to interview those who had witnessed my German childhood.

With the invention of the personal computer, the Internet, and the cell phone, research took on a whole new meaning. Information once inaccessible was now readily available at the stroke of a few keys and in my own home. Finding out pertinent information had become so much easier. I no longer had to physically go to the library or take copious handwritten notes. All the access I needed to discover the answers to just about anything was right at my fingertips.

One day in 2014, I received an e-mail from Hannelore typed in German. Using the Google Translate app, we were able to communicate in spite of the language barrier that had hindered us so many years ago on my last visit. I learned that both Mother and Father Webber, Hannelore's parents, had passed away years after my first visit. Ludwig Zimmermann, Else's husband and the father of her two sons, had lost his battle with lung cancer and died in 2006. Else had died shortly after in 2007.

Else had always been frightened that Helga would one day reveal her secret to Ludwig. Their mother-daughter relationship was based on hurt, anger, secrets, and lies, with Helga holding all the cards. Several years before his death, Helga secretly met with Ludwig and told him about Else's past life in Bingenheim. Returning home in a rage, driven by deep hurt and pain, he confronted Else. Obviously, it was a difficult time in their marriage. They considered divorce but ultimately opted to work on their marriage, making a commitment to stay together. Neither of them ever spoke about Else's daughters again.

No longer willing to hold on to the family secret, Helga had told not only Ludwig but also Else's two sons, Reinhard and Jürgen, shortly before Else's death. The older son had contacted Hannelore asking how to get in contact with me. Naturally, I was both surprised and delighted to hear of my half-brothers' desire to communicate. This was glorious news!

"Give them my e-mail address, please," I wrote in my response. Hannelore forwarded my e-mail address to Reinhard Zimmermann, Else's elder son.

Several days later, Reinhard introduced himself in an

e-mail with his photo attached. I was elated. I was gaining two half-brothers, along with some insight into our mother from two people who had known her quite well. For some reason, I felt the need to authenticate myself by e-mailing several pictures of my life in Germany with Else, Helga, and Imgard. He, too, sent pictures of his life with Else and their father. Through e-mail and the use of language translation, Reinhard shared how the secret of our existence was revealed beginning with a quick telephone conversation.

"Reinhard, I have something really important to tell you," Helga had said. "Can we meet?"

"Can't you tell me now?" he countered.

"No. My information is much too important to discuss over the phone. Besides, I haven't seen you in a while. We can have a chance to visit when we meet. What's a good day and time to meet?"

Reinhard, sensing the urgency in her voice, agreed to met with her several days later in her home. With tears in her eyes, Helga told Reinhard about Else's prior life in Bingenheim and of JoAnn's and my existence. She handed him a German newspaper clipping with the picture of me being held by Sister Mella, getting ready to board the plane to the United States. He was stunned, not knowing what to believe.

Naturally, he went directly to meet with Else at a local café, where he confronted her, repeating all that Helga had told him. Else simply stayed quiet, saying nothing.

"I tried talking to Mother about you girls," Reinhard told me, "but she denied Helga's claims and refused to talk, so I thought maybe it wasn't true, in spite of having seen pictures of you. Eventually, Else said, 'I don't know why Helga would tell such a lie,' with such indignation in her voice that I was convinced she was telling me the truth."

He put the matter aside. Soon after, Else was admitted to the hospital after tripping and falling, injuring a disk in her lower back. While in the hospital, she suffered an aneurysm, went into a coma, and died within a week of being admitted.

Shortly after Else's death, Reinhard began to wonder about his mother's past life. She had been a very secretive woman, never revealing anything about her life before her marriage to his father.

"Whenever we asked her about the past, our grandparents, life before us, she would scoff and change the subject, never answering our questions," Reinhard told me. Fearing that her secrets would be revealed, she spoke of nothing about her past, carrying her ancestry, her childhood, and her prior life to her grave.

Doubt began to creep into Reinhard's mind as a result of an encounter he'd had in 2006, months after his father's death. He received a short, handwritten letter requesting to meet over tea at a Frankfurt restaurant. The letter, signed by Ernst Claassen, a retired police officer who lived in Ehringshausen about a ninety-minute drive from Frankfurt, stated that he had very important information that he wanted to discuss with Reinhard. The letter seemed authentic, especially coming from an officer of the law, so Reinhard called the phone number given in the letter.

They made arrangements to meet shortly afterward. Ernst revealed that he was Else's firstborn child whom she had given up for adoption, leaving him at three days old to be raised in a Kinderheim until his adoption. His father was Else's one and only love, the Nazi soldier she had met during World War II. Being a police officer and having direct access to people's contact information, Ernst had contacted Else and arranged to meet her at a local Frankfurt coffee shop. Else had agreed, but changed her mind just before they went to enter the coffee shop together. She stopped at the doorway and, with disdain in her voice, said to him through clinched teeth, "You go your way and I'll go mine." Gesturing with her hand to shoo him away from her presence, she quickly turned and walked away, never to see or speak to him again.

Ernst, angry, hurt, and devastated by the sting of a second rejection by his birth mother, shared his painful story with Reinhard, confident that it would go no further. Ernst told Reinhard that his family didn't know that he was adopted, and he wanted to keep it a secret.

Determined to know my mother as a human being and to find answers to the lingering questions surrounding my adoption, I felt great joy when I began planning with Hannelore and Reinhard to visit Germany again. This time my visit would be to meet my newly discovered brothers, Reinhard and Jürgen, and Reinhard's partner, Fritz. I was especially excited to reconnect with Hannelore and my oldest sister, Helga.

* * *

On October 9, 2015, I arrived at the Frankfurt International Airport after an eighteen-hour flight with butterflies in my stomach in anticipation of meeting everyone. Fritz, Reinhard's partner of thirty-six years, was designated to meet me at the airport, as he spoke

English and had been included in all the correspondence between Reinhard and me. I recognized Fritz from the photo he had e-mailed before my arrival. He was warm, loving, and welcoming, giving me a bear hug that was reserved only for family. He helped me navigate through the maze of German directional signs and long walkways to the underground airport parking lot.

Fritz drove me to Bingenheim, where Hannelore now lived. Shortly after her mother's death, Hannelore had returned to her childhood home, the same house where Mother Webber had often looked after Imgard and me, and where I had visited her during my two-week trip to Germany in 1986. Hannelore greeted me with loving, open arms, giving me a kiss on both cheeks as she promptly duplicated the

Hannelore nee Webber-Prohaska

warm hug Mother Webber had given me so many years ago. I easily slipped into the role of "little girl" as I melted into her warm embrace.

Hannelore pampered me just as she had when she'd helped her mother care for my sisters and me when we were small. Jakob, her husband, was full of excitement as he spoke in German, his hands flying as he gestured nearly every word to ensure that I understood what he was saying. Few words were needed when each morning we greeted each other with "*Guten morgen,*" followed by a hug and a kiss on both cheeks. We were family who loved and respected each other. Hannelore had brushed up on her English enough to interpret what was being said as we met daily in her kitchen to eat and talk. With no consistent Wi-Fi accessible to me in the village, both of us held German-English dictionaries in our hands every time we tried to communicate.

We walked the village, catching up on our lives and filling in my absent memories of the life I had lived there. On one of our many walks, Hannelore informed me that I probably wouldn't see Helga this visit; she had decided she didn't want to see me. When asked for further details, Hannelore was hesitant to say much more, shrugging her shoulders with a look of "I'd rather not say." I didn't press the issue but thought it strange.

I was later informed that Helga was not pleased about my visit and had tried to dictate who would pick me up from the airport. Although ostensibly she wasn't interested, Helga called daily while we were having our morning coffee to inquire about our schedule and the status of my visit. I didn't think much of it at the time, simply brushing it off and telling myself that it wasn't personal. After all, I had done nothing to Helga, at least not from my perspective.

I savored every moment of my two weeks living, breathing, and sleeping in the village of my childhood, eager to listen to anyone who reminisced about my life shortly after World War II. As I took my daily walk, villagers would come out of their homes or lean out of their upstairs windows facing the street to reminisce about their experiences with my family during my brief years in Bingenheim. Although the "old-timers" didn't speak English, we somehow communicated through hand gestures, lots of finger pointing, and my ability to understand some German words. Imgard and I were the only two biracial babies in the village in the 1950s, which certainly had its advantage, as it ensured that my family and I would be remembered for years to come.

Several days after my arrival, Hannelore drove me to Frankfurt to meet for the first time my two brothers Reinhard and Jürgen. With no elevator in Reinhard's apartment building, we climbed the stairs to his fourth-floor apartment, arriving breathless but excited. While we caught our breath, I rang the doorbell and waited in anticipation. Fritz opened the door, grinning widely as my brother rushed past him to wrap his arms around me in the kind of hug a big sister treasures.

Reinhard, with short blond hair, blue eyes, and fair skin, had a smile that would light up any room. His gracious, outgoing, loving personality warmed my heart, striking down all hesitation as to how he would accept me. There would be no rejection from him. Reinhard told me that my brother Jürgen was unable to be there, as he was called to work that morning. Several days later, I met Jürgen, whose open arms and acceptance of me doubled my joy.

Fritz worked diligently to interpret all that we were saying as we sat around the dining room table sipping tea and talking about our lives and how we'd discovered each other. Reinhard excitedly presented many photos and documents they had discovered while clearing the home after Else's death. I too shared many old photos given to me by Earl that documented my existence with him and Else. My love for my brothers grew, as we talked nonstop, getting to know each other and realizing that we had similar extroverted personalities, which led quickly to our bonding. We also had similar growing-up stories, as Else had emotionally abandoned Reinhard as well.

Upon Else's death, Fritz and Reinhard bought a beautiful,

stately tree located in a government-owned forest cemetery. Instead of graves and tombstones, the forest provides a unique and cheaper alternative to the traditional grave. The ashes of the dead are buried in the family's privately owned patch of land surrounding the base of the tree. Reinhard and Fritz had bought a rather large tree plot to accommodate the cremated remains of five members of the Hilsheimer/Zimmermann family. The remains of Else and her husband, Ludwig Zimmermann, are the first to be buried under the family's tree.

As I rode to the site listening intently to Fritz and Reinhard's explanation of Else's grave, I had an urge to pinch myself to make sure I wasn't dreaming. I had met Else only once, in 1986, and had spent a few hours questioning her along with my sisters about our adoption. And now, twenty-nine years later, I was going to visit her grave. Arriving in the forest, my brothers and I began walking a well-manicured, paved walking path that climbed ever so slightly uphill. Goose bumps rose on my skin as I shivered from the cool, damp

Else's Forest Grave Site

morning air. Dew covered the lush, deep-green foliage, and tree leaves were waving at me as I walked the path. I lifted my face, looking up to see the power of the sun and savor its light among the forest shadows dancing across my face.

The beauty of the woods belied the sober purpose of our visit, but our surroundings soon took on a cemetery atmosphere as we continued to walk deeper into the forest. We arrived at a clearing designated for those who desired a cool drink of water from the wooden drinking fountain or simply needed to rest, leaning back on the six sturdy benches placed in the open area. We spotted plaques bearing various family names displayed on trees throughout our walk. The Hilsheimer/Zimmermann tree bore the family-name marker nailed to it at eye level. This was it. This was where our mother, Else's cremated remains were buried.

I stood there in silence as sadness filled my heart. Her peaceful burial site was in sharp contrast to the unsettling life she had lived. I was paying my respects to a mother who had given me life but then abandoned me, denying my very existence right up to her death. Although I grieved for our broken family, I couldn't summon up a daughterly feeling of mourning for a parent. She was a stranger, a shadow that lingered in the depths of my mind but lacked the positive emotional connection one would normally have for their mother. Else had left me; I had journeyed through life without her, and now I was standing by her grave with sadness for the life she had led and the secrets she had tried to carry to her grave.

Quietly, I walked away, knowing I would never visit her grave again. She was my birth mother who rejected me to the end of her days on this earth. I acknowledge that Else was my biological mother and I am her biological daughter, but it stops there. My mother was Mama, who was there for me through thick and thin, through my nightmares, my grief and loss, my successes and my failures. No one could ever take her place.

Life with Else hadn't been easy for Reinhard, I learned as

he shared his childhood memories with me during our two-hour drive back to Frankfurt.

"My constant feeling as a child was fear," he said. "She was a hard and bitter woman, frequently taking her aggressions out on me both physically and emotionally. When she was stressed, especially after a long day at work, I would get a spanking for every small thing I did. She would strike me with anything she could get her hands on—belt, carpet beater sticks, and sometimes her hand.

"I would often cry myself to sleep at night," he went on with pain in his voice. "I never felt she loved me. She often belittled me, refusing to talk to me for days at a time. We grew up with very few if any kisses or hugs from our mother. She showed little affection, even toward my father."

As he spoke, I thought about Imgard and the physical abuse she had endured at Else's hands. Our birth mother had not changed but had found a new victim in Reinhard. Because of the physical and emotional abuse he'd experienced, he left home at the age of eighteen, determined to find his own path in the world. Having married Fritz, his partner of thirty-plus years, and having built a successful career for himself, Reinhard had made the best of things. His decision to leave home at an early age served him well.

* * *

My stay was quickly coming to an end, but there was one more very important exploratory trip I needed to take before flying home: a visit to Kinderheim St. Josef. I rented a car for the same two-hour drive to Mannheim, Germany, that my sister and I had taken in Mrs. Grammer's black Cadillac more than sixty years ago. I prepared the night before, making sure I had all my pictures and documentation proving that I was one of their "brown babies" who resided there in the early 1950s. I drove alone through many different German villages and cities, noting that the bumpy, often-unpaved roads on which we had traveled so many years ago had been replaced by smoothly paved autobahns (freeways). My excitement grew as I considered the significance of this journey: Kinderheim St. Josef had played a very pivotal role in my life.

On arrival, I parked my car directly in front of the Kinderheim. The unassuming, beige three-story building was located in the middle of the block in between two equally large buildings that housed a variety of merchants' shops. The name St. Josef stood out in large, bold gray letters along with the building's address number on the pale stucco facade. There were tiled steps to climb before reaching the doorbell and intercom to the orphanage. I proceeded to the large blond oak front door.

Almost hidden from street view, an intercom buzzer sat snugly to the left of one of the door's windowed sidelight panels. I rang the bell and waited for a voice to answer, asking me to state my business. Instead there was silence as I stood there several minutes, not sure what to do next. I rang a second time, and then a third, becoming braver with each press of the button. Finally, after several more buzzes, I realized that no one was going to answer.

Kinderheim St. Josef-Mannheim, Germany

Anxiety began to creep in, in the form of butterflies once again in the depths of my stomach. Had I made this trip for nothing? Was someone ever going to answer the door? Would I get to see the place where I'd lived after Else had sent my sister and me away? I contemplated my next move. Now more intent than ever on entering "my building," I felt my attitude changing from uncertainty to determination. *I'll stay here until I get in*, I told myself.

I sat down on the top step of the Kinderheim, right in front of its beautiful blond wooden door. I waited and waited, shifting around frequently in search of a comfortable position on the cold tile.

An hour had passed when a woman carrying a large wicker lunch basket covered with a blue cotton cloth crossed the street, walking toward me. *Is she going to open the door?* I wondered as we made eye contact and smiled. I quickly stood up to get out of her way as she climbed the steps and reached out to ring the intercom.

I thought it was likely she spoke English, as most of the younger generation of Germans speak it quite well. When she pushed the button, I said, "I would like to get in the building with you, please." Without asking me any questions, she smiled as someone inside buzzed the door open and she gestured for me to follow her in.

Realizing the young woman did understand English, I explained the purpose of my visit.

"I used to live here," I told her as she put her basket down on her desk. "I am here from America researching my family tree, as I was born here in Germany and given up for adoption. I lived here for a time before I was adopted and sent to America. I'd like to speak to someone who can help me with questions I have."

Just as I finished my request, a gentleman, the director of the Kinderheim, walked out of his office with curiosity on his face. He approached me, introduced himself in fluent English, and shook my hand before escorting me to a conference room where I began to share my story as he took a few notes. I provided him with documentation and pictures of my sister and me. He left for a moment, then returned from his office and offered to give me a tour of the Kinderheim whose halls I had once waddled down as a two-year-old so many years ago.

Although the landscape had changed considerably from the 1950s to 2015, the original building was still there, along with newer additions added after World War II. Many children were currently living there, waiting to be adopted or to be reunited once their parents became financially stable again. I wondered as I walked the grounds how many abandoned children living there would get the same opportunity I had in being placed in a Christian family environment with loving parents who provided for them both physically and emotionally. I prayed that all the children there would find love, happiness, and peace.

My trip ended with the realization that I had just touched the surface of who Else truly was and there was much more to discover in order to answer the remaining questions. I had accomplished a lot in my two-week visit to Germany: meeting my brothers and Fritz, reconnecting with Hannelore and the many villagers who remembered me, keeping a daily journal in which I gathered firsthand information about my life from everyone who had information to share, visiting Else's grave, and touring the Kinderheim. With this phase of my journey of discovery complete, I flew home to America, already planning a return trip in 2017.

* * *

July 2017 came quickly, and I began packing for my return trip to Germany determined to complete my search for truth about Else, our life in Germany, and my adoption. A month living there would give me the time needed to reconnect with my family and acquaintances and to continue my research. My goal was to complete my interviews and information gathering before joining villagers, family, and friends in a two-day celebration of Hannelore's eightieth birthday. The first party was being held at Hannelore's home in Bingenheim.

I arrived in Germany on July 10, 2017, intent on completing my research before her birthday on August 1. Accommodating a visitor for thirty days would have been too much of a burden for anyone to handle, and especially for Hannelore just then, when she was working hard on organizing her birthday festivities. Staying at the Hilton Hotel in Frankfurt and renting a car gave me the freedom to continue my ancestry research and explore Germany without interfering in my family's daily routine. More importantly, it allowed me to spend more time with my brothers, who lived close to my hotel.

Several days before the celebration began, I made preparations to spend a few days in Bingenheim with Hannelore. Many of the villagers planned to join in the first day's celebration at her home. The evening before, I became her helper in preparing her patio for the big bash: setting up tables and chairs; placing tablecloths, stemmed wine and water glasses, and floral centerpieces; and sweeping the patio and brick walkway that led to her home shortly before the guests were to arrive.

The home phone rang as Hannelore, Jakob, her husband, and I were having tea before continuing our chores for the party. It was my sister Helga. In rapid German, Helga began to explain that she had no desire to see me and was angry that I would be attending the birthday party the following day. "What does she want anyway? Why is she here?" Helga demanded.

"She is here because I invited her here, Helga," Hannelore said.

"Ute hasn't spoken to Imgard in years! She is mean and cruel to her. I don't want to speak to her or be around her."

"How can that be, Helga?" Hannelore replied, a frown furrowing her brow. "Ute just showed me a picture of her son's wedding, and Imgard was there."

Feeling the pressure and realizing that Hannelore wasn't buying into the lie, Helga offered her last excuse, lashing out with anger and determination to hurt me, saying, "I still don't want to see or be around her. Ute is the reason Else gave us all away."

"Helga," Hannelore said, "I really want you to be at my birthday party. After all, we are sisters. I'm going to miss having you there."

"Well, maybe. Are my brothers going to be there tomorrow?" Helga asked.

"Yes, they will be at my home tomorrow, but not at the celebration at the center."

"Well, I don't know if I will come tomorrow," Helga hedged. "If I do, I will sit far away from her. I will not speak to her."

Helga had stated her position with finality in her voice. She curtly hung up the phone. Hannelore rejoined us at the table and relayed the conversation to me in English. I was stunned at Helga's accusations, realizing she was desperately trying to turn Hannelore against me by convincing her I wasn't who I seemed to be. We were all uncertain whether Helga would attend the next day.

Hannelore's eightieth-birthday festivities began on the first day with villagers stopping by to present a variety of gifts and then sit on her outdoor covered patio, partaking of refreshments and simply enjoying each other's company. The classic European atmosphere of light conversation, good wine, food, and taking lots of pictures brought pleasure to Hannelore. There were no cell phones out, no television blaring, and no music blasting so loudly you couldn't communicate with one another. Instead, the village choir, of which Hannelore is a member, sang beautiful songs, ending their short concert with the traditional "Happy Birthday" song before joining in the party. Throughout the afternoon, there was a steady stream of voices and laughter, with an occasional champagne toast to Hannelore by those newly arrived.

When guests first began to show up, Hannelore came inside the house, where I was washing dishes while viewing through the kitchen window the crowd gathering on the patio. Most who attended were the older villagers, who spoke no English but remembered my family and me living there many years earlier.

Hannelore leaned over and whispered excitedly in my ear, "Helga is outside on the patio. Go out there."

"Which one is Helga?" I asked. "What does Helga look like?"

Thirty-one years had passed since the last time I had seen her at our meeting with Else in 1986. Knowing how time ages all of us, I needed help in identifying her. Pointing toward a woman who stood talking with another guest, Hannelore took the dish towel out of my hands and guided me toward the door to the patio. Helga stood five-foot-two, plump, with short, dark brown bobbed hair and fair skin. She wore oversize, round-framed dark brown eyeglasses. I reached back in my mind but could not equate this older lady with the Helga I remembered meeting decades earlier.

I nervously exited the house onto the patio, nodding my head and saying hello to the guests. I noticed that Helga was no longer on the patio but had moved into the small guesthouse that was an extension of the patio and had been set up to accommodate the overflow of guests. Sitting at the very table I had helped prepare earlier was Helga, chatting in German with another guest. Helga did not hesitate in her conversation or acknowledge my presence, not even with a glance in my direction when I entered the room. She was aware of my presence simply by reading the face of the guest, who acknowledged me as I entered.

Although the guest spoke to me, Helga never turned her head toward me, made eye contact, or acknowledged in any way, even when I stood next to her. It was as if I didn't exist. I was caught by surprise, not expecting such a harsh and disrespectful public display of rejection. Trying to put my ego aside, I turned away to busy myself with the numerous tasks needed to keep the party flowing. *I will not make a scene and ruin Hannelore's birthday party*, I told myself. *I will do the same as Helga's doing and ignore her as well*. And yet, the wrenching pain of rejection settled deep in my soul.

As guests continued to arrive, I hugged and spoke to those I knew. Hannelore beckoned me to sit at the large table with some of her friends I had met and spent time with on my previous trip to Germany. Helga sat at a separate table in close proximity to mine. Sitting next to me was a retired schoolteacher who spoke very good English. As group dynamics would have it, he naturally slipped into the role of interpreter for our table. Helga was in my line of sight as I turned to talk with him. As people asked questions of me about my stay, he interpreted my answers. I noticed Helga leaning slightly in our direction, listening intently to grab onto as much information about me as possible. After all, she had been phoning Hannelore daily to be informed about our plans.

At one point, walking with a cup of coffee in her hand, Helga came over to the condiment table and deliberately reached right across my body for the cream as I stood there stirring my tea. We were close enough to touch, to smell each other's breath, but being just as stubborn as she, I turned my head and walked away, her eagle eyes following my every move. In that moment I could not bring myself to speak to her, to acknowledge her presence, as the pain of rejection and my ego took over, fearing public humiliation would follow the very public rejection she had just given me. I went along with the tone she had set, even though the core of me desired to behave differently. I wanted to speak, be cordial. After all, we were sisters. But Helga had made it very clear that "sisters forever" was not in the cards for her and me. She was determined to make sure everyone knew that *sisters* was not a word to be used to describe us. Her early departure from the afternoon birthday party helped to quiet my anxiety.

Many of the villagers were aware of the situation and had watched the dynamics unfold between us throughout the party, although I'd chosen to ignore Helga's coldness and focus my attention on Hannelore and her guests. Now, we had a second birthday party reserved for family and close friends the following day. Would Helga attend? Would the drama continue?

Hannelore's second birthday party took place in a neighboring village a short drive from Bingenheim, in a recreation center located on a large, scenic fishing pond. This intimate setting gave the group of invited family and friends a place to smoke or enjoy the fresh air outside along the lake, while inside the building was a bar and serving area

Hannelore's Birthday Party by the Lake

where piping-hot, homemade German food was served buffet style upon the arrival of all the guests.

Hannelore's son, daughter-in-law, and granddaughter arrived, along with many other family members and friends bearing gifts and their appetites. I was standing talking with Hannelore and a guest when Helga entered the room. To my surprise, she walked directly toward us, keeping her eyes locked on Hannelore as she entered our group's circle. Helga stopped, greeted Hannelore, and then fell silent. Someone in the group complimented Hannelore on the necklace and earrings she was wearing.

"This is a birthday present from Ute," Hannelore explained with a proud smile spreading across her face as her hand caressed the necklace lying gracefully around her neck.

Helga quickly turned, looking me up and down but avoiding any eye contact as her lips curled into a snarl. "*Idgitt*" (ugh), she said with disdain as she flipped her head upward quickly, then walked away in disgust. With Hannelore embarrassed and a look of surprise on the guest's face, I excused myself from the group and walked away to resume greeting the many guests who were quickly arriving. This was Hannelore's day, and I refused to ruin it for her simply to satisfy my ego and pride.

And yet the strained situation was weighing on Hannelore. Every few minutes she would seek me out to make sure I was feeling comfortable. Determined not to let Helga's hateful attitude and disrespectful behavior ruin the birthday celebration, I assured Hannelore that all was fine and that she had only to mingle with her guests and enjoy her birthday. Everyone present knew my family story and knew Helga was my biological half-sister who chose to ignore my very existence. They were watching me closely to determine my reaction to her highly public rejection of me. I knew in my head that I had done nothing wrong and could do nothing to change the situation. I felt the sting of rejection Helga intended to inflict on me, much like what our mother had inflicted on all of us.

Helga had given me an opportunity to truly put into

practice my core belief that man is basically good, but fear can drive us to be cruel to each other. To assure Hannelore I had not spoken hollow words, I continued greeting and conversing with the guests, relying on those who spoke English to interpret for those at the table who didn't. My strategy worked. Everyone began to feel comfortable as they laughed and talked freely, knowing nothing was going to happen to ruin the party atmosphere.

* * *

Rejection is to be expected as part of the process of searching to reconnect with someone from your past, especially in the search for biological parents or siblings. I still had one more sibling I needed to find before returning to America: my newest discovery, Ernst Claassen, my oldest half-brother and Else's firstborn, whom she had abandoned in the early 1940s during World War II. Googling his name, I had found numerous listings, but only one with the correct town of Ehringshausen an hour's drive from Frankfurt am Main. Excited but apprehensive, I plunged forward, knowing that it was highly likely that rejection by him was imminent.

Ernst had told Reinhard in 2006 that Else's abandonment of him was a secret that he kept from his family and friends. In spite of this revelation, using my GPS I took an early morning drive to his small village and parked my rental car along the curb directly in front of his family home. Feeling uncertain, I spotted a young neighbor and his wife several houses away sitting in chairs on their driveway, enjoying the beautiful sunny day. I got out of my car, approached them, and introduced myself, confident that they probably spoke at least some English.

"Good morning," I said. "I am looking for a Ernst Claassen who is a retired police officer. I have his address here and wanted to make sure he was still your neighbor before I approach his door."

"Yes. He is our neighbor," the man said. "He lives several houses down."

I thanked them and returned to my car debating with myself. *Should I ring his doorbell?* I knew the language would be a barrier, since Ernst spoke only German. Although I wanted to at least meet him once, I knew that he had been adamant in expressing to Reinhard that he didn't want any further contact with him or any part of Else's family lineage. *Am I selfish to want this so badly and ignore his wish?* I thought. *Will I ruin his family life forever by showing up?*

In an agony of uncertainty, sitting in my car parked right in front of his home, I debated for an hour before finally reaching the conclusion that I needed to back off. Rejection was to be respected, even though it was not a respectful act. I reluctantly drove away with deep sorrow in my heart, realizing that we would never meet. I would never even know what he looked like.

At my request, Reinhard spoke to Ernst over the telephone the following day, only to learn that he had been on vacation and hadn't been home the day I'd arrived in front of his house. He reiterated to Reinhard his desire to have no further contact with people from his past. Considering Else had given him up for adoption at birth and he had never known her or his siblings, it was understandable that he felt no connection to us. We were strangers to him, and the double rejection he'd experienced with our mother, at birth and many years later outside the Frankfurt café, contributed to his desire to put it all behind him.

Despite this unfavorable outcome, I had done the best I could to accomplish my mission of answering my lifelong questions. Reconnecting with family and friends who loved and cared about me while being rejected by those who did not feel a connection was all a part of the discovery process. The gift that was given to me at the end of the quest was discovering the answer to my question *Who am I?* I returned home to America feeling blessed, realizing that God's plan for me was the perfect plan. My curiosity about Else and why she'd made the decisions she had had been answered. I had fulfilled the promise I had made to myself so many years ago while struggling to write my sixth-grade English paper on the topic of family.

CHAPTER X

LOVE, FORGIVENESS, AND HEALING

"Forgiveness is not an occasional act,
it is a constant attitude."
—*Martin Luther King Jr.*

The loss of birth parents often stirs up feelings of grief and injury, regardless of whether the parent is dead or still alive. People grieve over the loss of their biological families, and I was no exception to this research-based finding. Having the added layer of being biracial and an international adoptee, the loss of my heritage and culture was an additional component. The need to know from where I came and to answer the question "Who am I?" is a healthy and natural curiosity for every human being.

Being abandoned by both birth parents had a dramatic impact on me as I progressed through life's many stages: marriage, the birth of children, divorce, and the deaths of loved ones. With each step, especially the birth of each of my children, came additional motivation to revisit my unanswered adoption questions. When I became a single parent who was responsible for raising two sons, I was determined not to continue the pattern of abandonment my birth mother had role-modeled for me so early in my life. I was determined to be the mother that she had not been to me.

As my two sons each reached the ages of two, five, and then eight, the ages I, JoAnn, and Helga had been when Else had walked away from us, I would find myself reflecting on the question *Could I ever walk away from my children and transfer my parental rights to strangers, never to see or know what happened to them?* I tried to imagine the reaction of my children at that age if I were to abandon them suddenly, leaving them with total strangers, never to see them again. I tried to imagine how I, as their mother, would feel to lose such a precious gift God had given me—a gift of unconditional love poured out daily by my innocent, lovable, often energetic boys.

I realize that many mothers who do make the agonizing decision to give up a child for adoption are genuinely doing so out of a deep and abiding love for them. Giving up a child so that he or she may have a better future is the demonstration of a mother's unselfish love. It is a decision that is not easily made and has repercussions for everyone who is involved in the process. Maybe under different circumstances, I might have chosen to give up my own children for adoption, but I was grateful that it was not something I had to wrestle with; it was not the path that opened for me.

The research of Evan B. Donaldson in a 2009 Adoption Institute study indicated that to develop an identity when adopted is much more challenging even in adulthood because of the many commonly unanswered questions adoptees have: *Why was I given up for adoption? What became of my birth parents? Do I have other siblings? Whom do I physically resemble? Whose personality did I inherit?* These questions we carry with us for the rest of our lives, or at least until we find answers to them.

Due to my unique circumstances in being biracial and an international adoptee, additional questions surfaced. *Why was she so willing to send us thousands of miles away from the country of our birth to a foreign land where we did not know the culture or speak the language? Did she give me up because my skin was too dark? Was my hair too woolly? Did she not love me?*

Although I don't recall the exact circumstances, I remember during my adolescent years hearing the statement "If your mother doesn't love you, no one will." It hit deep into the core of my being as I translated it into a single question: *Did my birth mother love me?* Knowing that she had abandoned me stirred up the emotions of fear and pain. But the fear of further rejection and the hurt that comes from that action did not deter me from having a deep and burning desire to search for the answer.

According to author Gary Chapman in his book *The Five Love Languages*, one of our primary emotional instincts is to be loved. We spend our daily lives being bombarded with love messages through advertisements on TV as well as through movies, poems, songs, plays, and magazines. It is our nature as human beings to seek love and to be genuinely loved by another. It validates us as human beings to have someone see us as a person who is worth loving.

Early attachments to our mothers give us a subconscious example of how relationships work in the world and demonstrate the meaning of love. From infancy until old age, connections to others, especially our mothers, build confidence and self-esteem, ensuring that we develop into healthy, whole adults. A powerful and detrimental force to reconcile is when the very person who brought you into the world, your mother, doesn't want you and doesn't love you.

The pain of rejection brings about deep sadness and anger, as it triggers conscious and subconscious hurt and painful memories. For many of us, abandonment equates to rejection, which translates into *She didn't love me, so she gave me up for adoption.* The fear of rejection is genuine in those who are searching to reconnect with their birth parents. Studies warn adoptees that about one percent of mothers who gave up a child for adoption have no desire to reconnect with their birth child. This type of rejection is doubly painful because it becomes the second time the birth mother rejects them.

My first and only meeting in adulthood with Else in Germany, alongside my sisters, was an intensely emotional experience. An emotional roller coaster of feelings accompanied this initial contact with Else. Her stoic demeanor sitting on the couch with her arms crossed as if to shield herself from our barrage of questions sent a clear message that she was an unwilling participant. Love, connection, and affection were absent even as she acknowledged that we were her children.

Meeting Else- 1986

When Else claimed that she had put us up for adoption because she'd repeatedly been fired from jobs once employers had learned that she had mixed-race children, her explanation sounded reasonable. History documents the racial climate during the 1950s as one in which Germany viewed all biracial babies, war babies, occupation babies as "a problem" that the German government and others needed to fix. Shipping us off to other countries for adoption was one acceptable solution at the time.

Although logic told me I was not the reason Else had walked away from her responsibilities as a mother, there is a part of me that must acknowledge some truth to the implied statement she made that my dark skin played a significant role in her decision to abandon me. There was no denying that race was a factor, if we believe Else was telling the truth. As she spoke, guilt-ridden questions of self-doubt and self-worth resurfaced in my mind, as they had so many times in the past. *Was my skin too dark? Was my hair too curly and unruly? Was I an embarrassment to her? Am I to blame for breaking up the family?*

Maya Angelou said it best: "When you know better, you do better." These are powerful words that allow people to make a mistake and hopefully learn from it. Knowledge and role-modeling behavior, we learn first through our parents and then through others. Growing up in an unhealthy relationship environment in which her alcoholic father physically abused her mother left Else with a lack of understanding of what a healthy love relationship entails. The failure of Rudolf and Liba to demonstrate what passionate and unconditional parental love entails severely hindered Else's ability to develop healthy love relationships with her own children. She did not have the knowledge or experience to pass the lessons of love on to her offspring. You cannot give what you don't have.

Reinhard confirmed my analysis of our mother when he spoke to me with sadness as he reminisced about how our mother had raised him.

"Else wasn't an affectionate person," he said. "I don't ever remember either of my parents hugging or kissing each other. I'm not sure if she was ever happy. She rarely showed us any affection, like most mothers show their children. But she was nicer to my brother than she was to me." He concluded assessing his home life by saying, "She was a harsh and bitter woman."

The added insight into Else's parental track record spoke more of the truth of why she gave Imgard and me up for adoption than any of the excuses she gave when we met at Hannelore's home in Frankfurt. Having given birth to six children, Else abandoned four of us, walking away each time to begin a new life as a single, childless woman. The abandonment of her children wasn't based on race but rather on convenience.

This pattern of abandonment when difficulty arose began with Ernst, who was the first to be left behind at three days old in the hospital in Frankfurt in 1942. My sister Imgard at five years old and I at two followed the same fate when Else abandoned us to Mrs. Grammer and the Kinderheim St. Josef in 1952. Our sister Helga experienced a similar fate later that same year when, months after we were taken, Else left her at the babysitter's home and never returned to pick her up.

Else made decisions based on what she thought was best for her and her alone, regardless of who else was affected.

This kind of selfish thinking was role-modeled early in her life by her father when he abandoned her after her mother was forcibly sent to die in a concentration camp. Else's inability to be a nurturing, loving, and caring mother drove her decision to give all of us away. *Did she love me?* My research concluded the answer to be no. I don't believe my birth mother loved anyone but herself.

Scientific research today has proven that while in the womb, babies hear and smell their mother, feel her emotions, and will know her voice once they are born. Separation from the birth mother may not be consciously remembered but will leave indelible abandonment fears that most adoptees grapple with throughout their lives. Because of the breach of the most critical relationship in life—that with our mother— the grieving of loss begins when we are separated from her. These psychological issues stemming from abandonment threaten our emotional well-being in a variety of ways, but most commonly undermine our ability to develop emotional connections such as self-esteem, romantic relationships, and motherhood, to name a few.

My own abandonment issues show up in my deep-seated insecurities masked by a facade of self-reliance, extreme independence, and a goal-driven mind-set. The need to feel safe and connected to loving people is a basic need, but the fear of being let down by others is more significant, which kept me focused more on my career goals than on developing meaningful relationships. Relying on myself ensured that I would get the job done! Being self-reliant and independent of others allowed me to be in complete control and diminished the fear of being hurt or let down. After all, my birth mother had let me down; therefore, I was determined not to let anyone else do the same.

While self-esteem is a judgment made about oneself, it is strongly influenced by others, especially those we value in our lives. When those we value reject us, our self-esteem sinks as we question our value to others and to ourselves. The subconscious thoughts and feelings of "less than" became the driving force in proving to my birth parents that it would have been worth their effort to have kept me. Even if they never knew, I would show them simply through my knowing I was successful in spite of their abandonment and my early childhood challenges.

I am proud of my accomplishments. Becoming a wife at seventeen and a mother twelve days after turning eighteen was a scary way to enter adulthood. Determined to become a success and a positive role model for my sons, I forged ahead, focusing on motherhood and completing my education. I attended Bakersfield Community College riding the city bus and sometimes pedaling my bicycle as a means of transportation until I acquired a secondhand car. Determined to earn my college degree, I graduated with a bachelor of arts degree in social science from California State University, Bakersfield, and a year later was awarded a California Lifetime Teaching Credential in secondary education.

While financially supporting my family as a classroom teacher, I continued my education, earning a master's degree in education administration and an Administrative Credential from the University of La Verne, in La Verne, California. With both sons no longer living at home, I worked in my district school office under the title of Director of Youth Support Services, and on school sites as dean of students, vice principal, and principal, retiring after thirty-four years of service in the field of education.

As I look back at my career accomplishments, I realize how my feelings of "less than" created a strong determination to become a successful, self-reliant mother and career woman. Feelings of vulnerability that lurked just below the surface of my facade kept me focused and determined not to have to rely on anyone to take care of my family or me. The traumatic decision made by my birth mother left indelible subconscious terrors that propelled the need to control certain things in my life. Daddy once told me, "No one ever lifts a finger to help you because you walk around with an independent, 'I got it under control' attitude." I often think about his assessment of me when I reflect on the image I project to others. I was a driven and focused high school student, mother, college student, and career woman intent on controlling my destiny.

Although I have been successful in my career, I have not been so in my love relationships. I chose men who lacked honesty, trustworthiness, and commitment. It simply wasn't who they were at the time of our relationships. The cycle of abandonment continued throughout my life, as I chose partners who treated me in much the same way my birth mother had. Just as Else had put her needs before those of her children, I subconsciously selected men who made choices based on their own desires and ignored the harmful emotional consequences their actions would have on me and the relationship.

I was deeply in love, and they professed the same; however, their behavior spoke otherwise. They often cheated on me with other women, yet I suppressed my pain, reluctantly returning to the same relationship after having received numerous apologies and promises to "never do it again," only to have the betrayal recur six to twelve months later. The pain of staying in a dysfunctional relationship was more bearable than the pain of letting go. I avoided letting go in spite of the detrimental effects on my self-esteem.

Along with the healing process comes the willingness to look in the mirror, giving oneself the opportunity for self-discovery and a deeper self-understanding. It was imperative that I acknowledge that I might have a hand in soliciting and inviting their actions by simply allowing myself to be mistreated. The nature of my affliction was that the fear of abandonment was so great, I chose men who I subconsciously knew would eventually abandon me. This familiar pattern was one that I could rely on and knew how to react to—just like my experience with my birth mother. The fear of being abandoned or let down by people I encountered throughout my life resulted in poor decision-making.

Releasing and letting go of a toxic relationship is essential in reaching peace. Knowing who we are as we make sense of our life experiences helps us to reach our higher potential. Reflecting on and understanding those experiences reveals who we are so that we can make positive changes. When we acknowledge and let go of our destructive behaviors, we become better human beings. I have learned that when one door closes, another opens.

In spite of my numerous insecurities punctuated by periodic boosts of confidence, I was determined to push through the toughest of obstacles to become a better person. Reading and studying about adoption and all that it entails prepared me for whatever might happen in the discovery of my birth parents. Professional counseling and reading about lessons learned by others provided me the emotional tools necessary to complete my journey toward forgiveness and healing.

* * *

Adoption remains an essential aspect of identity throughout an adopted child's adulthood. Most people, whether adopted or not, at some point ask themselves the age-old question *Who am I?* Forming our identities begins in childhood and progresses more intensely during adolescence and on into adulthood. Having been adopted creates obstacles in the search for one's own identity. Of all the questions I wanted answered, the top three were *Who am I? Why did you give me up for adoption?* and *Did you love me?* They were the foundation for all the other questions that needed answering.

The research of L. DiAnne Borders, Judith Penny, and Francie Portnoy in 2000 was my guide, providing the benchmark steps toward my healing. Their research identified five phases of adoptive identity that occur throughout our adulthood:

- *No awareness:* The adopted person does not outwardly acknowledge adoption issues.

- *Emerging awareness:* The adopted person views adoption as a positive influence and recognizes some issues but is not ready to explore these issues.

- *Drowning in awareness:* The adopted person has feelings of loss, anger, and sadness about the adoption.

- *Reemerging from awareness:* The adopted person recognizes the issues related to adoption but sees the positive aspects and is working toward acceptance.

- *Finding peace:* The adopted person has worked through their issues with the adoption and is moving toward peace and acceptance.

The quality of our life is often determined by how we respond to the events in our life. Taking on the role of a victim has no purpose in my life. I have chosen to forgive all who have rejected me, denying my very existence and in effect telling me loud and clear, "You don't matter." I want instead to focus on the positive aspects of my world. My journey of self-discovery and the process of writing this book have helped me significantly to complete my quest for wholeness as I moved through the various stages, finally reaching the last stage of "finding peace."

I am blessed to have been adopted by parents who provided me a warm, loving home, coached me on how to navigate through the norms and cultures of my two worlds, and provided me with the best educational opportunities available. Daddy and Mama raised me to be honorable, kind, focused, committed, and civic-minded as they role-modeled those same qualities in their own lives.

They played a significant role in shaping me into the person I have become today. Daddy showed me what was possible to achieve, as he was a living example of how a person with little formal education but common sense and a willingness to work long and hard hours could achieve his goals. Mama showed me how to be a mother, homemaker, and leader, and strive to live daily by my Christian principles. I am forever grateful to them for having adopted me.

My most important personal achievement was to break the

cycle of abandonment begun by my grandparents and carried forward by my birth mother, Else. By staying focused as a single parent on raising two smart, handsome, and successful grown sons, I believe I have broken the family cycle of abandonment. The focus on family is paramount in our family dynamics. All of us make sure work and career never overshadow the importance of the bonds we have worked so hard to establish. Family is first.

During my search for love, healing, and forgiveness, I quickly realized that my life story wasn't going to be all wine and roses but rather a mixture of the good, the bad, and the ugly secrets of a family torn apart by one decision made by a single person. As I progressed deeper into the family, I discovered that all of us siblings had experienced similar emotional issues after Else, our birth mother, had made life-altering decisions that turned our entire lives upside down without warning.

With my odyssey completed, I have forgiven those who have brought me pain along my journey. My search and discovery of love, forgiveness, and healing have brought me to the stage of peace.

Family Picture 1950- Helga, Else, holding me, Imgard

CHAPTER XI

THE DISCOVERY OF YOU

"The fullness of life lies in dreaming and
manifesting the impossible dreams."
—Sri Chinmoy

I hope you will be encouraged to search for and learn about your roots even if you were not adopted. For those who have been, I hope reading my story will prompt you to embark on your own journey of discovery to meet your biological parents, siblings, and other family, while realizing that there may be disappointments along the way.

Acceptance of another person is a silent message backed by behavior that signifies that you're okay with them unconditionally. Keep in mind that rejection is always a possibility from any family member you discover. There may be some who will accept you and others who will reject you. I experienced both rejection and acceptance.

The rejection by my birth mother was an adjustment, but working with my professional counselor helped me to see Else for who she was and the limits of her emotional giving. I had hoped that all of my siblings shared with me the same desire to reconnect, but that was not the case. The two oldest siblings, Ernst and Helga, through their actions and words, made it clear that each of them would reject any further attempt to connect. His rejection of all his siblings and Helga's rejection of me during my later visits to Germany were rooted in the hurt and pain they experienced very early in life when they themselves were abandoned by our mother.

Their decisions to reject me saddened me deeply, forcing me again to work through the intense emotions of rejection and loss of family. In spite of this terrible disappointment, I remained steadfast and focused on my goal of building the family connections I could and strengthening my own identity as a result. This process requires determination in not letting anyone or anything stand in the way of self-discovery.

Hannelore Prokaska, the Bingenheim villagers who remembered me, and my birth father, Earl Laughton, were my saving graces in writing this book. They all accepted me with loving, open arms, filling in the gaps of my life story and helping me understand my German heritage and culture. Their support and my deeper awareness of my background empowered me and raised my self-esteem.

Veteran of Three Wars

Meeting my brother Reinhard, his partner Fritz, and my brother Jürgen brought closure to my family circle. Their warmth, openness, and love were evident at the first meeting as we hugged and held each other, realizing we were connected not only by our DNA but also by our inner spirit. I am blessed to have them in my life still, as I visit Germany every other year. I'm also grateful to continue the relationship with Earl, "Pops," who resides in the United States.

In your discovery, it is imperative to view the life-altering decision made for you from a variety of perspectives. It is essential that you consider the decision maker's point of view, their circumstances, the time during which they lived, and their state of mind at the time of the decision.

I encourage anyone interested in ancestral discovery or the search for birth parents first to read a variety of recent research on discovering your ancestry, adoption, and foster placement. Learning more about such topics as abandonment, connection, reconnection, and other related issues will assist you on your path. The Internet, libraries, and local adoption agencies all have resource materials, mostly free, that will help you in your search.

It is essential to be prepared with tools in your "toolbox of life" to use throughout the process if you choose to pursue it. Hitting a few emotional snags is inevitable, as emotions will run high. Be prepared for the rejection you may experience from your siblings, other relatives, and even your birth mother. Having resources readily available, such as a professional counselor who will help talk you through some of the emotional challenges you'll encounter along the way, is essential to your well-being. Your search is a very personal journey that only you can venture on, but you do not have to cope with it alone.

Below are a few suggested tactics to try, websites to explore, and things to keep in mind. I hope they will help you along the road to discovery.

1. Look up these groups focused on adoption and related issues:

   - The ALMA Society (formerly Adoptees' Liberty Movement Association; almasociety.org)

   - adoption.com

   - International Soundex Reunion Registry (isrr.org)

   - Reunion Registry (reunionregistry.org)

   - American Adoption Congress (americanadoptioncongress.org)

   - Bastard Nation (bastards.org)

   - Binti (binti.com)

   - Concerned United Birthparents (cubirthparents.org)

   - National Center on Adoption and Permanency (ncap-us.org)

2. Explore social media sites, such as Facebook, Twitter, LinkedIn, and Instagram.

3. Create a Facebook page and e-mail address specifically dedicated to your search.

4. Contact the adoption agency or lawyer that handled your adoption.

5. Learning about your DNA can be helpful. Try

   - ancestry.com

   - 23andme.com

- ancestrydna.com

- familytree.com

6. Find a record of your birth certificate through local online courthouse records or americanadoptioncongress.org, or you can physically go to your local records office.

7. Remember, most birth mothers are not open to facing the past, confronting the pain, or tackling the reality of having given you up for adoption. Your approach and the wording of your questions when you make the initial contact may determine whether you receive a positive or negative outcome. Avoid asking questions in an accusatory tone.

8. Adoptees have a right to contact anyone, including their birth mothers.

9. Building relationships is a slow process. Give it time. Realize you are developing a "get acquainted" relationship first, hoping to develop it into a friendship. Time and life experiences make it unlikely that you will develop a parental relationship. You can only have a relationship with a willing participant.

10. Be prepared for rejection by your birth mother. Having a counselor who can help you sort out your feelings of hurt is essential throughout this journey.

11. Remember you are not alone. Joining adoption blogs and grief-and-loss group sessions or merely attending church may give you much-needed support.

12. Join the many adoption registries online. Google "adoption registry."

For anyone who has been abandoned, put up for adoption, or simply raised by someone other than your mother, I encourage you to attempt to uncover your roots, to undertake your own quest to locate and meet any living biological parents, siblings, and extended family, while keeping in mind that you may encounter disappointments along the way. The search will provide you the opportunity to experience new peace and freedom upon unearthing the good, the bad, and sometimes the ugly truth that often lies buried in the family history. Through this process, you may find it in your heart to forgive those who have brought hurt and pain into your life. My fervent wish is that you will find love, forgiveness, and healing as you complete your own journey of discovery.